The News Portal Publisher's Handbook

MASTERING NEWS PORTAL PUBLISHING

A Comprehensive Guide to
Launching, Growing, and
Innovating in the Digital
Media Landscape

OSMAN KARAKAS

About Book

Book Title: **Mastering News Portal Publishing**

A Comprehensive Guide to Launching, Growing, and Innovating in the Digital Media Landscape

Format: Word/PDF

Size: 6X9 inches - 15.24X22.89 cm

Total Pages: 257

E-mail: okarakas@hotmail.com

Web: www.osmankarakas.com

CONTENTS

4

Preface:

In an era where information flows at the speed of light and media landscapes undergo constant transformation, the role of news portals has never been more critical. These digital platforms are the gateways through which society gains access to news, opinions, and insights, shaping public discourse and illuminating the world's complexities.

"**Mastering News Portal Publishing**" is born out of a profound appreciation for the vital role that news portals play in our information age. It's a journey through the intricate web of digital journalism, from inception to innovation, and every milestone in between. As we embark on this adventure together, we aim to equip you, the reader, with the knowledge, strategies, and tools needed to navigate this dynamic and ever-evolving landscape.

Within these pages, you'll find a treasure trove of insights, drawn from the experiences of industry experts, successful news portal publishers, and those who've navigated the challenges of this digital frontier. Whether you're an aspiring publisher ready to embark on your own digital journey or a seasoned professional seeking to adapt and thrive in a constantly changing environment, this guide has something valuable to offer you.

Our aim is to provide you with a comprehensive roadmap that covers the essential facets of news portal publishing. From the inception of your portal, understanding the intricacies of the news industry, and setting realistic expectations, to assembling the right team, optimizing your portal for performance, and forging partnerships with news agencies—each chapter is designed to empower you.

In the world of news portal publishing, innovation is the lifeblood that sustains growth and relevance. That's why we delve deep into fostering a culture of innovation, adapting to shifting trends, engaging with your audience, and ensuring the long-term sustainability of your portal.

Our journey also explores the ethical responsibilities of journalism, the power of multimedia storytelling, the art of promotion in the digital realm, and the influence of social media. Through the stories of both successful and closed news portals, you'll gain valuable insights into the dos and don'ts of the trade.

We understand that the digital landscape can be daunting, but it's also teeming with opportunities. As you read through these pages, we encourage you to reflect on your own path, adapt the knowledge you gain to your unique circumstances, and chart a course toward a successful and ethical news portal that informs, engages, and enlightens its audience.

This guide is more than a compilation of information; it's a companion on your journey—a trusted advisor offering insights and guidance every step of the way. We invite you to immerse yourself in the world of news portal publishing, explore the nuances of this ever-changing field, and embark on a path that combines journalistic integrity with digital innovation.

Welcome to "**Mastering News Portal Publishing**," where the future of digital journalism unfolds, one page at a time.

Welcome to the world of news portal publishing.

Osman Karakas

Chapter 1: Introduction to News Portal Publishing

Section 1.1: Understanding the News Industry

In the digital age, the news industry stands at a crossroads, where traditional print media has given way to the dynamic world of online news portals. This transformation has led to several critical developments:

The Shifting Landscape of News

The traditional model of news delivery through newspapers and television networks has undergone a seismic shift. Declining readership and viewership of traditional media have coincided with the rise of online news portals. This shift in consumer behavior has redefined how news is produced, consumed, and shared.

As readers increasingly turn to online sources for news, the role of print newspapers and television broadcasts has evolved. Traditional media outlets are adapting by establishing their own digital presence, but the competition is fierce. Understanding the evolving dynamics of news consumption is crucial for news portal publishers to carve their niche in the digital landscape.

The Digital Revolution

The advent of the internet has democratized access to information. The digital revolution has not only accelerated the speed of news delivery but has also allowed for a diversity of voices and perspectives. However, it has also led to concerns about the credibility of sources and the spread of misinformation.

Online news portals have harnessed the power of multimedia content, including videos, infographics, and interactive elements, to engage readers in new ways. This transformation has blurred the lines between traditional journalism and citizen journalism. Recognizing the impact of this digital revolution on the news ecosystem is vital for staying relevant and resonating with modern audiences.

News Consumption Habits

To succeed in news portal publishing, it's essential to grasp the changing habits of news consumers. This includes understanding how people access news, which platforms they prefer, and what types of content resonate with them. An in-depth knowledge of audience behavior is crucial for tailoring your content strategy.

Today's readers consume news on an array of devices, from smartphones to tablets. Mobile news apps and social media platforms have become primary sources of information. As algorithms play a significant role in content discovery, publishers must adapt their content for optimal visibility. Additionally, understanding the psychology behind news consumption can guide publishers in crafting compelling and shareable content.

The Role of News Portals

News portals have become central players in the news ecosystem. They curate, create, and disseminate information across various digital platforms, providing readers with diverse perspectives and timely updates. As a news portal publisher, you will occupy a pivotal role in connecting significant events with your audience.

The agility of online news portals enables real-time reporting, live coverage, and multimedia-rich storytelling. Engaging readers through interactive features, comments sections, and social media integration is crucial for building a loyal readership. In this era of information abundance, the role of news portals extends beyond reporting to providing context, analysis, and a sense of community.

Ethics and Responsibility

With the power to influence public opinion comes great responsibility. News portals have a moral and ethical duty to practice journalism that upholds the highest standards of truth, accuracy, and fairness.

Journalistic integrity is the cornerstone of credibility. Upholding these principles involves rigorous fact-checking, source verification, and adherence to ethical guidelines. It also encompasses transparent correction of errors and the responsible handling of sensitive information. In a world where misinformation can spread rapidly, ethical journalism serves as a beacon of trust and reliability.

Understanding these foundational aspects of the news industry is essential for anyone entering the world of news portal publishing. It provides a solid grounding that will serve as the basis for navigating the complexities and opportunities that lie ahead in your journey.

Section 1.2: Why Start a News Portal?

In a world inundated with information, the decision to start a news portal is a significant one. It's not just about joining the digital media landscape; it's about becoming a voice of influence and insight. This section explores the compelling reasons why individuals and organizations embark on the journey of news portal publishing:

1. Be the Source of Truth and Credibility

In an era characterized by information overload and the rapid spread of misinformation, the role of trustworthy news sources has never been more critical. Starting a news portal allows you to be a beacon of truth and credibility in a sea of uncertainty. Your commitment to rigorous fact-checking, ethical journalism, and transparency can establish your news portal as a trusted source for your audience.

2. Address Unmet Information Needs

Every community and demographic has unique information needs that traditional media might not fully cater to. Starting a news portal enables you to address these unmet needs. Whether it's hyper-local news, niche topics, or underrepresented perspectives, your portal can fill the gaps in the news landscape and provide value to specific audiences.

3. Advocate for Causes and Issues

News portals have the power to advocate for causes and issues that matter. Whether it's environmental conservation, social justice, or healthcare reform, your platform can serve as a rallying point for like-minded individuals and organizations. Advocacy journalism can bring about positive change and foster a sense of community among your readers.

4. Amplify Diverse Voices

News portals offer a platform to amplify diverse voices and perspectives. You can prioritize inclusivity by featuring underrepresented voices, minority communities, and marginalized groups. By doing so, your portal becomes a catalyst for social change and a space for dialogue on pressing issues.

5. Embrace Digital Innovation

The digital realm is a playground for innovation in journalism. Starting a news portal allows you to explore new storytelling formats, interactive features, and multimedia content. You can experiment with data journalism, immersive storytelling, and user-generated content, enhancing the reader experience and setting your portal apart.

6. Build Your Brand and Influence

A news portal is not just a platform for news; it's a brand in itself. By consistently delivering quality journalism and building a loyal readership, you can elevate your portal's brand and influence. Your portal can become a recognized authority in its niche or geographic region, attracting partnerships and opportunities.

7. Adapt to Changing Media Trends

Traditional media models have faced disruptions, but news portals are well-positioned to adapt to changing media trends. As consumer preferences shift towards digital and mobile platforms, news portals can pivot quickly to cater to these trends. Staying nimble and responsive to evolving audience behaviors is a key advantage.

8. Entrepreneurial Opportunities

Starting a news portal offers entrepreneurial opportunities. It allows you to build a digital business around your passion for journalism. You can explore revenue models such as advertising, subscriptions, sponsored content, and events.

Entrepreneurship in digital media can be both personally fulfilling and financially rewarding.

9. Fill the Information Void

In regions where traditional news outlets have downsized or closed, there may be an information void. Starting a news portal in such areas can provide a lifeline of information to the community. You become a vital source of local news and a catalyst for community engagement.

10. Contribute to Public Discourse

A news portal contributes to public discourse and democratic processes. It provides a platform for informed debates, discussions, and analysis. By fostering a space for civic engagement, your portal plays a crucial role in shaping public opinion and influencing decision-making.

These are just a few of the compelling reasons why individuals and organizations choose to start news portals. The decision to embark on this journey is not to be taken lightly, but it offers the opportunity to make a meaningful impact in the world of journalism and beyond.

Section 1.3: Setting Realistic Expectations

Launching a news portal is an exciting endeavor, but it's essential to set realistic expectations to ensure your journey is both fulfilling and successful. This section delves into various aspects of managing expectations when entering the world of news portal publishing:

1. Understanding the Learning Curve

Starting a news portal involves a learning curve, especially if you're new to journalism or digital media. Setting realistic expectations about this curve is crucial. You'll need time to familiarize yourself with content management systems, digital tools, and journalistic practices. Embrace this learning process as an investment in your portal's future success.

2. Managing Content Workflow

Content creation and management can be more complex than anticipated. Setting realistic expectations about the time and effort required to produce quality news content is essential. Balancing the need for speed with editorial standards is an ongoing challenge. Developing efficient content workflows and collaboration processes is key to maintaining consistency and quality.

3. Building an Audience Takes Time

Gaining a substantial readership doesn't happen overnight. It's important to set realistic expectations about audience growth. Your portal will likely start with a small, dedicated readership. Building a larger audience requires consistent content production, effective marketing, and engagement strategies. Patience is essential as you gradually expand your reach.

4. Revenue Generation Challenges

Monetizing a news portal can be challenging, especially in the early stages. Setting realistic expectations about revenue is crucial. Advertising revenue, subscriptions, and sponsored content may take time to materialize. Diversifying revenue streams and exploring partnerships can help sustain your portal as it grows.

5. Navigating Competition

The digital news landscape is highly competitive. Setting realistic expectations about competition is important. Recognize that you'll be vying for readership with established news outlets and other newcomers. Focus on what makes your portal unique and strive for differentiation in content, style, or niche.

6. Adapting to Technology Changes

Technology evolves rapidly, impacting how news is consumed and delivered. Setting realistic expectations about adapting to technological changes is vital. Be prepared to regularly update your portal's design, features, and compatibility with emerging devices and platforms to remain relevant.

7. Handling Criticism and Feedback

Constructive criticism and reader feedback are integral to improvement, but they can also be challenging to manage. Setting realistic expectations about handling criticism is essential. Embrace feedback as an opportunity for growth while also developing resilience to manage inevitable criticisms that come with public exposure.

8. Balancing Workload and Burnout

Launching and running a news portal can be demanding. Setting realistic expectations about workload and potential burnout is crucial for your well-being. Establish work-life balance practices, delegate tasks where possible, and seek support from a team or contributors to prevent burnout.

9. Tracking and Adjusting Goals

As your news portal evolves, your goals may need adjustment. Setting realistic expectations about goal tracking and flexibility is important. Regularly assess your portal's performance, audience feedback, and revenue metrics. Be prepared to pivot and adapt your strategies based on these insights.

10. Celebrating Milestones

Amid the challenges, it's essential to set realistic expectations for celebrating milestones. Recognize and celebrate your portal's achievements, whether it's reaching a specific readership milestone, winning an award, or receiving positive feedback. These celebrations can boost morale and motivation.

Understanding and managing these realistic expectations is integral to your journey in news portal publishing. It allows you to approach challenges with resilience, celebrate successes, and continually evolve your portal for long-term success.

Chapter 2: Necessities for Launching a News Portal

Section 2.1: Legal and Regulatory Considerations

Before embarking on your journey to launch a news portal, it's essential to navigate the complex landscape of legal and regulatory considerations. This section provides a comprehensive overview of the crucial aspects you must address:

1. Defining Your Legal Structure

The first step in navigating legal considerations is to define the legal structure of your news portal. Will it be a sole proprietorship, partnership, LLC, or corporation? Each structure has distinct implications for liability, taxation, and ownership. Consulting with legal professionals specializing in media law is invaluable for making informed decisions.

2. Intellectual Property Rights

Understanding intellectual property rights is paramount in journalism. Set realistic expectations about copyright laws, fair use, and intellectual property ownership. Ensure your writers and content creators are aware of copyright regulations when using third-party content, images, and multimedia elements. Create internal guidelines for proper attribution and permission when needed.

3. Libel and Defamation Laws

Libel and defamation claims are significant concerns for news portals. Setting realistic expectations about these legal risks is essential. Journalists must adhere to rigorous fact-checking and verification processes to minimize the risk of publishing defamatory content. Implement editorial guidelines and review processes to maintain accuracy and fairness in reporting.

4. Privacy and Data Protection

Privacy regulations, such as GDPR and CCPA, impact news portals' collection and handling of user data. Setting realistic expectations about compliance with these regulations is vital. Ensure you have clear privacy policies and mechanisms for obtaining user consent for data processing. Regularly update and audit your data handling practices to remain compliant.

5. Content Regulation and Obscenity Laws

News portals must be aware of content regulation and obscenity laws in the regions they operate. Set realistic expectations about adhering to these laws. Develop content guidelines and editorial standards that align with legal requirements. Keep abreast of changes in content regulation and be prepared to adapt your practices accordingly.

6. Shield Laws and Source Protection

Shield laws vary by jurisdiction but generally protect journalists from being compelled to reveal their sources. Setting realistic expectations about the limitations and scope of these laws is essential. While they offer protection, they may not cover every situation. Develop internal policies for source protection and educate your team on the nuances of these laws.

7. Advertising and Sponsored Content Guidelines

Monetizing your news portal through advertising and sponsored content requires adherence to advertising standards and guidelines. Setting realistic expectations about transparency and disclosure in advertising is vital. Clearly label sponsored content and adhere to advertising industry standards to maintain credibility and trust among readers.

8. Accessibility Compliance

Web accessibility is a legal requirement in many regions. Setting realistic expectations about accessibility compliance is crucial. Ensure your news portal is accessible to individuals with disabilities, including those with visual or auditory impairments. Regularly conduct accessibility audits and address any issues to remain compliant.

9. International Operations and Jurisdiction Challenges

If your news portal operates internationally, you'll encounter jurisdiction challenges. Set realistic expectations about the complexities of international law and regulations. Consult legal experts with international expertise to navigate issues such as cross-border content distribution, data privacy, and foreign legal claims.

10. Handling Legal Disputes and Litigation

Despite precautions, legal disputes may arise. Setting realistic expectations about handling legal disputes and potential litigation is essential. Establish protocols for addressing legal challenges, including retaining legal counsel, responding to cease and desist letters, and pursuing dispute resolution methods such as arbitration or mediation.

Navigating the legal and regulatory landscape is a critical aspect of launching and operating a news portal. Engaging legal counsel with expertise in media law is highly recommended to ensure compliance, mitigate risks, and protect the integrity of your news portal.

Section 2.2: Choosing a Niche and Audience

Selecting the right niche and understanding your target audience is a pivotal step in the successful launch of a news portal. This section explores the multifaceted aspects of making this critical decision:

1. Identifying Your Passion and Expertise

Choosing a niche begins with identifying your passion and expertise. What topics or subjects do you have a genuine interest in and knowledge of? Set realistic expectations about the importance of personal passion because it will sustain your dedication throughout the journey. If you're passionate about a subject, it's more likely to resonate with your audience.

2. Researching Market Trends

Setting realistic expectations about market trends is essential. Conduct thorough research to understand current trends and emerging topics within your chosen niche. Use analytics tools to identify keywords and content gaps that offer opportunities for coverage. Staying informed about market dynamics allows you to position your portal strategically.

3. Evaluating Audience Demand

Audience demand is a crucial consideration when selecting a niche. Setting realistic expectations about your target audience's preferences, needs, and behaviors is vital. Conduct audience surveys, analyze competitor data, and engage with potential readers to gain insights into what they're looking for in news content. Your niche should align with audience interests.

4. Assessing Competition

Competitor analysis is a part of setting realistic expectations. Evaluate existing news portals in your chosen niche. Identify gaps in their coverage, areas where you can offer a unique perspective, or underserved audience segments. Understand the competitive landscape to position your portal effectively.

5. Balancing Broad vs. Narrow Niches

Setting realistic expectations regarding the breadth of your niche is important. Broad niches cover a wide range of topics, while narrow niches focus on specific subtopics or industries. Consider your capacity to cover the chosen niche comprehensively. A narrow niche can lead to a highly engaged, specialized audience, while a broad one offers more diverse content opportunities.

6. Audience Segmentation

Audience segmentation is a strategy for setting realistic expectations about reaching specific reader demographics. Divide your target audience into segments based on factors like age, interests, location, and behavior. Tailor your content and engagement strategies to address the unique needs of each segment, maximizing reader engagement.

7. Content Strategy and Differentiation

Set realistic expectations about your content strategy and how you'll differentiate your portal within the chosen niche. Develop editorial guidelines that align with your niche's tone and style. Consider content formats, such as articles, videos, and infographics, that resonate with your audience. Plan how you'll offer fresh perspectives and unique angles in your reporting.

8. Scalability and Long-Term Viability

Consider scalability when choosing a niche. Setting realistic expectations about your portal's growth potential is crucial. Ensure that your chosen niche allows for long-term viability and adaptability as market dynamics evolve. A niche with room for expansion or diversification can help sustain your portal's growth.

9. Audience Engagement and Community Building

Setting realistic expectations about audience engagement is essential. Consider how you'll build a sense of community around your portal. Engage with readers through comments, forums, or social media platforms. Foster a two-way dialogue to create a loyal readership base.

10. Monitoring and Adaptation

Finally, setting realistic expectations about the need for ongoing monitoring and adaptation is crucial. Stay agile and be prepared to adjust your niche or content strategy based on audience feedback and evolving trends. Regularly review your analytics to measure the effectiveness of your niche selection and audience engagement efforts.

Choosing the right niche and audience is a pivotal decision in launching a successful news portal. It's a combination of personal passion, market analysis, audience understanding, and a commitment to delivering valuable content that sets the stage for long-term success.

Section 2.3: Developing a Business Plan

A well-structured business plan is the foundation of a successful news portal. This section explores the intricacies of creating a comprehensive business plan that encompasses all essential aspects of your venture:

1. Defining Your Vision and Mission

The starting point of your business plan is defining a clear vision and mission for your news portal. Set realistic expectations about the importance of these guiding statements. Your vision articulates the long-term goals and impact you want to achieve, while the mission outlines your portal's purpose and how it serves your audience. These statements provide a compass for decision-making.

2. Market Analysis and Research

Setting realistic expectations about the need for market analysis is vital. Your business plan should include thorough research on your chosen niche, target audience, and competitors. Understand market trends, audience behaviors, and content gaps. Identify opportunities and challenges that inform your portal's strategy.

3. Revenue Model and Monetization Strategy

Setting realistic expectations about revenue is essential. Outline your revenue model and monetization strategy in your business plan. Consider multiple income streams, such as advertising, subscriptions, sponsored content, events, and merchandise. Calculate revenue projections based on realistic assumptions and industry benchmarks.

4. Budgeting and Financial Projections

Financial planning is integral to setting realistic expectations. Develop a detailed budget that covers initial startup costs, ongoing operational expenses, and revenue projections. Factor in personnel costs, technology investments, marketing, and legal expenses. Use financial modeling to estimate profitability and cash flow.

5. Audience Growth and Engagement Strategies

Setting realistic expectations about audience growth and engagement is crucial. Detail your strategies for attracting and retaining readers. Include plans for content creation, marketing campaigns, social media engagement, and community building. Define key performance indicators (KPIs) to measure the success of your strategies.

6. Editorial Guidelines and Content Strategy

Your business plan should set realistic expectations for your editorial guidelines and content strategy. Outline your approach to content creation, including topics, formats, and publication schedules. Emphasize the importance of adhering to journalistic ethics, accuracy, and editorial standards to build reader trust.

7. Marketing and Promotion

Setting realistic expectations about marketing and promotion is vital for gaining visibility. Develop a comprehensive marketing plan that includes digital marketing strategies, social media promotion, SEO optimization, and outreach to potential partners and collaborators. Allocate resources and timelines for each marketing initiative.

8. Technology and Infrastructure

Your news portal's technology and infrastructure are essential components. Set realistic expectations about the technology stack, content management system (CMS), hosting solutions, and security measures. Ensure scalability and reliability to accommodate growth.

9. Team and Talent Acquisition

Setting realistic expectations about team development is crucial. Outline your team structure, roles, and responsibilities in the business plan. Determine whether you'll hire journalists, editors, designers, developers, and sales or marketing professionals. Consider both in-house and freelance contributors.

10. Risk Assessment and Mitigation

Setting realistic expectations about risk assessment and mitigation is essential for business continuity. Identify potential risks such as legal challenges, audience attrition, or revenue fluctuations. Develop contingency plans and risk mitigation strategies to address these challenges.

11. Sustainability and Growth

Your business plan should set realistic expectations for sustainability and growth. Define milestones and key objectives for your portal's growth over time. Include plans for expanding your audience, diversifying revenue streams, and adapting to market changes.

12. Timeline and Milestones

A timeline with realistic milestones is essential to track progress. Create a timeline that outlines key activities, deadlines, and milestones, from the initial concept to the portal's launch and beyond. This visual representation helps you stay on course and adjust strategies as needed.

A well-crafted business plan serves as a roadmap for your news portal's success. It not only helps you set realistic expectations but also provides a strategic framework for decision-making, resource allocation, and growth. Regularly review and update your business plan to adapt to changing circumstances and opportunities.

Chapter 3: Assembling Your Team

Section 3.1: Identifying Key Roles

Building the right team is a critical step in the successful launch and operation of a news portal. This section explores the key roles you need to identify and their responsibilities:

1. Editorial Leadership

Setting realistic expectations about editorial leadership is essential. Identify the individual or individuals responsible for the editorial direction of your news portal. This role encompasses defining content strategy, upholding journalistic ethics, overseeing content production, and maintaining editorial standards. Editorial leaders shape the portal's voice, style, and credibility.

2. Journalists and Writers

Journalists and writers form the core of your content creation team. Setting realistic expectations about their roles is crucial. These individuals are responsible for researching, writing, and editing news articles, features, and reports. They should possess strong writing skills, journalistic integrity, and the ability to meet deadlines.

3. Editors

Editors play a vital role in maintaining the quality and accuracy of content. Setting realistic expectations about their responsibilities is important. Editors review articles for grammar, style, and factual accuracy. They ensure that content aligns with editorial guidelines and ethical standards. Editors also collaborate with writers to improve content quality.

4. Technical Team

Setting realistic expectations about your technical team is essential, especially if your news portal has a digital focus. This team includes web developers, designers, and IT professionals. They are responsible for website maintenance, user experience, responsive design, security, and technology integrations. A well-functioning technical team ensures a seamless online presence.

5. Marketing and Outreach Specialists

Marketing and outreach specialists are critical for gaining visibility and attracting readers. Setting realistic expectations about their roles is vital. These professionals develop and execute marketing strategies, manage social media accounts, optimize content for search engines, and engage with the audience. They play a crucial role in audience growth.

6. Sales and Advertising Team

If your revenue model involves advertising or sponsored content, setting realistic expectations about the sales and advertising team is essential. This team identifies potential advertisers, negotiates partnerships, and manages ad campaigns. They work closely with the editorial team to ensure that sponsored content aligns with your portal's values and audience.

7. Community Managers

Community managers are responsible for fostering engagement and building a loyal readership. Setting realistic expectations about their role is important. They moderate comments, forums, or social media interactions, ensuring a respectful and constructive environment. Community managers also collect and relay reader feedback to improve the portal.

8. Legal and Compliance Experts

Legal and compliance experts play a crucial role in navigating the legal aspects of news publishing. Setting realistic expectations about their responsibilities is vital. They provide legal counsel on libel, copyright, privacy, and content regulations. They draft contracts, review content for legal risks, and help your portal stay compliant with laws and industry standards.

9. Business and Financial Professionals

Setting realistic expectations about your business and financial professionals is essential for sound financial management. These individuals manage finances, budgets, financial projections, and revenue generation strategies. They ensure the portal's financial stability and growth.

10. Data and Analytics Specialists

Data and analytics specialists help you make data-driven decisions. Setting realistic expectations about their roles is crucial. They track audience metrics, analyze user behavior, and provide insights to optimize content, marketing, and audience engagement strategies. Their work contributes to audience growth and content performance.

11. Contributing Writers and Experts

Contributing writers and experts can provide diverse perspectives and niche knowledge. Setting realistic expectations about their role involves identifying individuals who can contribute specialized articles, op-eds, or insights. Collaborating with subject matter experts enhances your portal's credibility and breadth of coverage.

12. Interns and Junior Staff

Interns and junior staff can be valuable additions to your team. Setting realistic expectations about their roles involves providing training and mentorship opportunities. They can assist with research, fact-checking, content creation, and administrative tasks, contributing to the portal's efficiency.

Identifying these key roles and their responsibilities is essential for building a well-rounded team that can execute your news portal's vision effectively. Setting realistic expectations for each role ensures that team members understand their contributions and align with the portal's mission.

Section 3.2: Hiring Journalists and Editors

Journalists and editors are the heartbeat of your news portal, responsible for producing high-quality, credible content. This section delves into the process of hiring and nurturing these essential team members:

1. Identifying Core Competencies

Setting realistic expectations about the core competencies of journalists and editors is essential. Identify the skills and qualities you seek in candidates. These may include strong research and writing abilities, news judgment, adherence to journalistic ethics, attention to detail, and the ability to work under deadlines.

2. Crafting Job Descriptions

Creating well-defined job descriptions is crucial for setting realistic expectations. Clearly outline the roles and responsibilities of journalists and editors. Specify the type of reporting they'll be responsible for (e.g., breaking news, features, investigative journalism) and any specialized knowledge or beats required.

3. Conducting a Comprehensive Search

Setting realistic expectations about the hiring process is important. Conduct a thorough search for candidates. Advertise job openings on relevant job boards, journalism associations, and your news portal's website. Encourage referrals and networking within the industry. Ensure that your search reaches a diverse pool of talent.

4. Portfolio and Writing Samples

Evaluating portfolios and writing samples is integral to setting realistic expectations. Request candidates to submit their portfolios and samples of their work. Assess the quality of their writing, the depth of their research, and their ability to cover diverse topics effectively. Look for candidates with a track record of factual and balanced reporting.

5. Interviews and Auditions

Interviews and auditions help set realistic expectations about candidates' abilities. Conduct in-depth interviews that assess their journalism skills, ethics, and compatibility with your portal's values. Consider asking candidates to complete a written assignment or provide a sample article to evaluate their writing proficiency.

6. Assessing Ethical Standards

Setting realistic expectations about ethical standards is paramount in journalism. During interviews, explore candidates' understanding of journalistic ethics and their commitment to accuracy, fairness, and impartiality. Ask about their approach to handling sensitive topics and ethical dilemmas.

7. Editorial Judgment

Assessing candidates' editorial judgment is crucial. Set realistic expectations about their ability to prioritize news stories, evaluate sources, and make editorial decisions. Present scenarios and ask how they would approach various editorial challenges, demonstrating their critical thinking and news judgment.

8. Collaboration and Adaptability

Setting realistic expectations about collaboration and adaptability is important. Journalists and editors must work closely with colleagues, sources, and stakeholders. Evaluate candidates' interpersonal skills, their ability to work in a team, and their willingness to adapt to changing news priorities.

9. Diversity and Inclusion

Setting realistic expectations for diversity and inclusion is essential. Consider the importance of diverse perspectives and voices in journalism. Strive to hire journalists and editors from varied backgrounds and experiences to ensure comprehensive and inclusive coverage.

10. Onboarding and Training

Onboarding and training are critical for setting realistic expectations. Provide new hires with a comprehensive orientation that includes an overview of your portal's mission, values, and editorial guidelines. Offer training on tools, technology, and newsroom processes.

11. Mentorship and Professional Development

Setting realistic expectations for mentorship and professional development is essential for nurturing talent. Pair junior journalists with experienced mentors who can provide guidance and support. Encourage ongoing learning and opportunities for growth to retain top talent.

12. Diversity of Perspectives

Diversity of perspectives is vital for setting realistic expectations. Foster an environment that encourages journalists and editors to bring their unique viewpoints and ideas to the newsroom. Encourage open dialogue and collaboration to enrich your portal's content.

Hiring journalists and editors is a critical step in building a strong news portal team. Setting realistic expectations throughout the hiring process ensures that you bring on board individuals who align with your portal's mission, values, and commitment to ethical journalism.

Section 3.3: Building a Technical Team

A technical team is the backbone of your news portal's digital presence. This section explores the intricacies of building a technical team that can manage your website, infrastructure, and digital operations effectively:

1. Roles and Expertise

Setting realistic expectations about the roles and expertise needed in your technical team is essential. Identify the key roles, such as web developers, designers, system administrators, and IT specialists. Each role should align with specific responsibilities, whether it's front-end development, server management, security, or design.

2. Technical Proficiency

Assessing technical proficiency is integral to setting realistic expectations. Candidates for your technical team should have the necessary skills and experience. Web developers should be proficient in programming languages like HTML, CSS, JavaScript, and have experience with content management systems (CMS) such as WordPress or custom solutions. Designers should demonstrate expertise in user interface (UI) and user experience (UX) design.

3. Problem-Solving Abilities

Setting realistic expectations about problem-solving abilities is vital. Technical team members should have a knack for troubleshooting and resolving issues promptly. Evaluate candidates' problem-solving skills by presenting them with real or hypothetical technical challenges they might encounter in maintaining your news portal.

4. Collaboration and Communication

Collaboration and effective communication within your technical team are essential for setting realistic expectations. Technical roles often involve working closely with non-technical colleagues, such as journalists and editors. Ensure that your technical team can explain complex technical concepts in layperson terms and collaborate seamlessly across departments.

5. Staying Current with Technology

Setting realistic expectations about staying current with technology is crucial. The digital landscape is constantly evolving, and your technical team must keep up with the latest trends, security updates, and emerging technologies. Encourage ongoing learning and professional development to ensure that your news portal remains technologically competitive.

6. Scalability and Redundancy

Scalability and redundancy are factors to consider when building your technical team. Setting realistic expectations about your portal's growth potential and the need for redundancy in case of server failures or technical issues is vital. Plan for scalability in infrastructure design and ensure that your technical team can handle increased traffic and data demands.

7. Security Expertise

Security is paramount for a news portal. Setting realistic expectations about the need for security expertise is crucial. Your technical team should have a deep understanding of web security practices, including protecting against DDoS attacks, securing user data, and implementing SSL certificates. Regular security audits and updates are essential.

8. Mobile Optimization

Setting realistic expectations about mobile optimization is important in the age of smartphones. Ensure that your technical team can optimize your portal for mobile devices, providing a seamless user experience across different screen sizes and resolutions.

9. Content Management System (CMS) Expertise

If your news portal uses a CMS, setting realistic expectations about CMS expertise is essential. Whether it's WordPress, Drupal, or a custom-built solution, your technical team should be proficient in managing and customizing the CMS to suit your portal's specific needs.

10. Regular Maintenance and Updates

Setting realistic expectations about regular maintenance and updates is crucial for the smooth operation of your news portal. Your technical team should have a schedule for routine maintenance, including software updates, security patches, and server optimizations.

11. Disaster Recovery and Backup Plans

Setting realistic expectations about disaster recovery and backup plans is vital. Your technical team should have robust plans in place to recover from unforeseen events, such as server crashes or data breaches. Regularly test these plans to ensure their effectiveness.

12. Collaboration with Non-Technical Teams

Collaboration with non-technical teams is essential for setting realistic expectations. Technical team members should be able to work closely with journalists, editors, marketing professionals, and others. Effective communication and understanding of the newsroom's needs are critical for success.

Building a skilled and reliable technical team is foundational to the success of your news portal. Setting realistic expectations regarding roles, technical proficiency, problem-solving, and collaboration ensures that your technical team can effectively support your portal's digital operations.

Chapter 4: Hosting Your News Portal

Section 4.1: Selecting a Reliable Hosting Provider

Choosing the right hosting provider is crucial for the performance and security of your news portal. This section delves into the factors to consider when selecting a reliable hosting provider:

1. Types of Hosting

Setting realistic expectations about the types of hosting is vital. Hosting providers offer various options, including shared hosting, virtual private servers (VPS), dedicated hosting, and cloud hosting. Assess your portal's resource requirements, traffic expectations, and budget to choose the most suitable type.

2. Reliability and Uptime

Setting realistic expectations about uptime is essential. Hosting providers should offer high uptime guarantees (99.9% or higher). Verify the provider's track record by reading reviews and checking their historical uptime performance. Downtime can lead to lost readers and revenue.

3. Scalability

Scalability is a key consideration. Setting realistic expectations about your portal's growth is vital. Ensure that the hosting provider can accommodate increasing traffic and data demands without compromising performance.

Scalability options may include easy upgrades or access to cloud resources.

4. Data Center Locations

Setting realistic expectations about data center locations is important. Choose a hosting provider with data centers strategically located to reduce latency and improve website loading times for your target audience. Consider global content delivery networks (CDNs) for wider reach.

5. Security Features

Security is paramount for a news portal. Setting realistic expectations about security features is crucial. The hosting provider should offer robust security measures, including firewalls, intrusion detection systems, SSL certificates, and regular security updates. Verify their approach to data protection and compliance with industry standards.

6. Backup and Disaster Recovery

Setting realistic expectations about backup and disaster recovery is vital. Ensure that the hosting provider offers automated daily backups and provides options for manual backups. Assess their disaster recovery plans and data restoration processes in case of unexpected issues.

7. Technical Support

Technical support is essential for setting realistic expectations. Hosting providers should offer responsive and knowledgeable customer support.

Consider factors such as available support channels (chat, email, phone), response times, and 24/7 availability. Efficient support can resolve issues promptly.

8. Pricing and Billing

Setting realistic expectations about pricing and billing is important. Compare hosting providers' pricing structures and understand the total cost of ownership, including any hidden fees. Consider long-term affordability, renewal rates, and scalability costs.

9. Content Management System (CMS) Compatibility

If your news portal uses a CMS, setting realistic expectations about CMS compatibility is essential. Ensure that the hosting provider supports your chosen CMS, whether it's WordPress, Drupal, Joomla, or a custom solution. Check for one-click installations and optimizations for your CMS.

10. Load Balancing and Redundancy

Setting realistic expectations about load balancing and redundancy is crucial. Hosting providers should offer load balancing solutions to distribute traffic evenly and prevent server overload. Redundancy measures, such as mirrored servers and failover systems, enhance reliability.

11. Performance Optimization

Performance optimization is key for user experience. Setting realistic expectations about performance optimization includes features like content caching, Content Delivery Networks (CDNs), and server-level optimizations. These measures improve page load times and responsiveness.

12. Reviews and Recommendations

Before finalizing your choice, setting realistic expectations about reviews and recommendations is essential. Research hosting providers thoroughly by reading user reviews, seeking recommendations from peers, and checking their reputation within the web hosting industry.

13. Terms of Service and SLA

Setting realistic expectations about terms of service and Service Level Agreements (SLAs) is vital. Review the hosting provider's terms and SLA carefully to understand their commitments regarding uptime, support, data privacy, and dispute resolution.

14. Migration Assistance

If you're transferring your portal from another host, setting realistic expectations about migration assistance is important. Some hosting providers offer migration services to ensure a smooth transition without data loss or downtime.

Selecting a reliable hosting provider is a critical decision in the success of your news portal. Setting realistic expectations about the factors mentioned above ensures that your hosting choice aligns with your portal's performance, security, and growth needs.

Section 4.2: Domain Registration and Management

Your domain is your news portal's digital identity. This section explores the intricacies of domain registration and management:

1. Choosing a Domain Name

Setting realistic expectations about choosing a domain name is essential. Your domain name should reflect your news portal's identity, be easy to remember, and relevant to your content. Consider factors such as brand consistency and search engine optimization (SEO). Check the availability of your desired domain name.

2. Domain Extensions

Setting realistic expectations about domain extensions is important. Domain extensions, also known as top-level domains (TLDs), include common options like .com, .net, and .org, as well as newer extensions like .news or country-specific TLDs (.uk, .ca). Choose a TLD that aligns with your portal's purpose and audience. Consider securing multiple relevant TLDs to protect your brand.

3. Registration Process

The domain registration process involves setting realistic expectations about the steps required. You'll need to provide personal or organizational information, including contact details, during registration. Some domain registrars may offer additional services like privacy protection to shield your contact information from public WHOIS records.

4. Domain Pricing

Setting realistic expectations about domain pricing is crucial. Domain registration fees can vary widely based on factors like the domain extension and registrar. Expect an annual renewal fee to maintain ownership of your domain. Some registrars may offer discounted initial registration fees.

5. Ownership and Control

Setting realistic expectations about ownership and control is vital. When you register a domain, you become its owner. Ensure that you have full control over domain settings, including DNS (Domain Name System) configuration, email forwarding, and subdomain management. Keep records of your domain registrar login credentials.

6. Renewal and Expiry

Setting realistic expectations about renewal and expiry is important. Domains typically require annual renewal to maintain ownership. Ensure that you set up renewal reminders and keep payment information up to date. Failure to renew a domain can result in its expiration and potential loss.

7. DNS Configuration

DNS configuration is integral to setting realistic expectations. You'll need to point your domain to your hosting provider's DNS servers. Understand how to update DNS records for your domain, including A records (for website hosting), MX records (for email), and CNAME records (for subdomains or redirects).

8. Transfer and Authorization Codes

Setting realistic expectations about domain transfers is essential. If you ever need to transfer your domain to a different registrar, you'll require an authorization code (also known as an EPP code or transfer code). Ensure that you have access to this code and understand the transfer process.

9. Domain Privacy Protection

Setting realistic expectations about domain privacy protection is crucial for your personal or organizational information. Some registrars offer domain privacy services that shield your contact details from public WHOIS records, reducing the risk of spam or unwanted contact.

10. Domain Portfolio Management

If you plan to manage multiple domains, setting realistic expectations about portfolio management is important. Consider using a domain management platform or registrar that allows you to centralize and efficiently manage all your domains, including renewals and updates.w

11. Legal Considerations

Setting realistic expectations about legal considerations is vital. Ensure that your chosen domain name doesn't infringe on trademarks or copyrights. Consult legal counsel if you have concerns about domain disputes or ownership issues.

12. Domain Security

Domain security is paramount. Setting realistic expectations about domain security involves enabling domain locking, two-factor authentication (2FA), and monitoring for any unauthorized changes or transfers. Protecting your domain from unauthorized access is crucial.

Securing and managing your domain effectively is an essential part of establishing your news portal's online presence. Setting realistic expectations regarding domain selection, ownership, renewal, and security ensures a smooth and secure digital identity for your portal.

Section 4.3: Security and Backup Solutions

Security and backup solutions are critical aspects of hosting your news portal. This section explores the intricacies of safeguarding your portal's data and operations:

1. Website Security

Setting realistic expectations about website security is paramount. Your news portal is vulnerable to various online threats, including hacking attempts, malware, and DDoS attacks. Choose a hosting provider that offers robust security measures, such as firewalls, intrusion detection systems, and regular security updates.

2. SSL Certificates

Setting realistic expectations about SSL certificates is crucial for user trust. SSL (Secure Sockets Layer) certificates encrypt data exchanged between your portal and visitors, ensuring secure connections. Ensure that your hosting provider offers free or affordable SSL certificates, especially if your portal handles user logins or transactions.

3. Regular Software Updates

Setting realistic expectations about regular software updates is essential. Outdated software, including your CMS, themes, and plugins, can be exploited by attackers. Stay vigilant about applying security patches and updates promptly to protect against vulnerabilities.

4. Security Audits and Vulnerability Scanning

Conducting security audits and vulnerability scanning is integral to setting realistic expectations. Regularly assess your portal's security with the help of security experts or tools. Identify and address vulnerabilities proactively to prevent security breaches.

5. Backup Solutions

Setting realistic expectations about backup solutions is crucial for data protection. Your news portal's content and databases should be regularly backed up to secure data against accidental deletion, hardware failures, or cyberattacks. Choose a hosting provider that offers automated backup solutions and store backups in secure offsite locations.

6. Disaster Recovery Planning

Setting realistic expectations about disaster recovery planning is vital. Prepare for worst-case scenarios, such as server crashes or data breaches. Develop a comprehensive disaster recovery plan that outlines the steps to recover data, restore services, and communicate with stakeholders in case of emergencies.

7. Data Retention Policies

Setting realistic expectations about data retention policies is essential for compliance and security. Establish clear policies for data retention, deletion, and archiving. Ensure that user data is handled in accordance with privacy regulations, and communicate your policies to users transparently.

8. User Authentication and Access Control

Setting realistic expectations about user authentication and access control is crucial. Implement strong authentication methods for user logins, especially for administrators. Use role-based access control (RBAC) to restrict access to sensitive areas of your portal, ensuring that only authorized personnel can make changes.

9. Monitoring and Alerts

Setting realistic expectations about monitoring and alerts is vital. Implement monitoring tools that track server performance, security incidents, and website traffic. Configure alerts to notify your team of unusual activities, potential breaches, or performance issues in real time.

10. Incident Response

Setting realistic expectations about incident response is essential. Develop a clear incident response plan that outlines the steps to take in the event of a security breach. Assign roles and responsibilities for incident management, and establish communication protocols for informing affected parties.

11. Compliance and Regulations

Setting realistic expectations about compliance and regulations is crucial. Stay informed about data protection laws and industry-specific regulations that may apply to your news portal. Ensure that your security practices align with these requirements to avoid legal issues.

12. Employee Training

Setting realistic expectations about employee training is important. Educate your team, including journalists and technical staff, about security best practices, phishing awareness, and data handling procedures. Security is a collective responsibility, and well-informed employees can help prevent security incidents.

13. Third-Party Security Audits

Setting realistic expectations about third-party security audits is important for transparency. Consider hiring independent security firms to conduct regular audits of your portal's security measures. External audits provide an unbiased assessment of your security posture.

Security and backup solutions are integral to safeguarding your news portal's operations and data. Setting realistic expectations regarding these measures ensures that your portal remains resilient in the face of evolving cyber threats.

Chapter 5: Selecting the Right Script/Theme

Section 5.1: Evaluating Content Management Systems (CMS)

Choosing the right Content Management System (CMS) is a critical decision in building your news portal. This section delves into the factors to consider when evaluating CMS options:

1. Understanding CMS Basics

Setting realistic expectations about understanding CMS basics is vital. Begin by grasping the fundamental concept of a CMS. It's a software application that allows you to create, manage, and publish digital content, including articles, images, videos, and more. Familiarize yourself with how a CMS simplifies content editing and organization.

2. Open Source vs. Proprietary CMS

Setting realistic expectations about CMS types is important. CMS options fall into two broad categories: open source and proprietary. Open-source CMS, like WordPress and Drupal, are freely available and highly customizable. Proprietary CMS, such as Adobe Experience Manager, often offer more advanced features but come with licensing costs. Assess your budget and specific needs to determine which type suits your portal.

3. Scalability

Setting realistic expectations about scalability is essential. Your CMS should accommodate your portal's growth. Evaluate whether the CMS can handle increasing content volume, user traffic, and additional features. Scalability ensures that your news portal can expand without major disruptions.

4. Customization and Themes

Setting realistic expectations about customization is crucial. Assess the CMS's flexibility in terms of design and functionality. Many CMS platforms offer a range of themes and templates, but the ability to customize these to match your portal's branding and unique requirements is essential.

5. Ease of Use

Setting realistic expectations about ease of use is important, especially if you have a team of journalists and editors. A user-friendly CMS simplifies content creation, editing, and publishing. Test the CMS's interface to ensure that your team can navigate it comfortably.

6. Community and Support

Setting realistic expectations about community and support is vital for troubleshooting and updates. Popular open-source CMS platforms often have active communities of developers and users who contribute plugins, themes, and support. Proprietary CMS may offer dedicated customer support. Assess the availability of support channels and documentation.

7. SEO Friendliness

Setting realistic expectations about SEO friendliness is crucial for online visibility. Your CMS should support SEO best practices, including customizable permalinks, meta tags, XML sitemaps, and mobile optimization. Evaluate how well the CMS facilitates SEO efforts to improve your portal's search engine rankings.

8. Mobile Responsiveness

Setting realistic expectations about mobile responsiveness is essential in the mobile-centric era. Ensure that your chosen CMS and theme are mobile-friendly, providing an optimal user experience on various devices and screen sizes.

9. Content Workflow and Collaboration

Setting realistic expectations about content workflow and collaboration features is important for newsrooms. News portals involve multiple contributors and editors. Assess whether the CMS supports content approval workflows, user roles, and collaboration features that streamline the editorial process.

10. Security

Setting realistic expectations about security is paramount. Your CMS should have a strong security track record. Regularly updated CMS platforms often address security vulnerabilities promptly. Implement additional security measures, such as secure login practices and user authentication, to safeguard your portal.

11. Multilingual Support

Setting realistic expectations about multilingual support is important if you plan to reach a global audience. Evaluate whether the CMS can handle multiple languages and localization features, enabling you to publish content in different regions and languages.

12. Accessibility Compliance

Setting realistic expectations about accessibility compliance is crucial for inclusivity. Ensure that your CMS adheres to accessibility standards (e.g., WCAG) to make your portal usable for individuals with disabilities.

13. Integration Capabilities

Setting realistic expectations about integration capabilities is essential. Determine whether the CMS can integrate with third-party tools, such as analytics platforms, email marketing software, and social media management tools, to streamline your portal's operations and audience engagement.

14. Total Cost of Ownership (TCO)

Setting realistic expectations about the total cost of ownership is vital. Consider both initial setup costs and ongoing expenses, including hosting, plugins, themes, and potential development or customization. Calculate the TCO to align with your budgetary constraints.

Evaluating and selecting the right CMS is a foundational step in building a successful news portal. Setting realistic expectations regarding the factors mentioned above ensures that your chosen CMS aligns with your portal's content, scalability, and user experience needs.

Section 5.2: Custom vs. Premium Themes

Choosing the right theme for your news portal is a crucial design decision. This section explores the differences and considerations between custom and premium themes:

1. Custom Themes

Setting Expectations for Custom Themes

Custom themes are tailor-made designs created specifically for your news portal. Setting realistic expectations about custom themes involves understanding the advantages and complexities:

Advantages of Custom Themes

- **Unique Branding**: Custom themes offer unparalleled uniqueness. Your news portal's design aligns precisely with your brand identity, making a memorable impression on readers.

- **Tailored Functionality**: Expect themes that cater to your specific needs. Custom themes can integrate unique features, layouts, and functionality tailored to your content and audience.

- **Optimized Performance**: Custom themes can be optimized for your portal's performance requirements, ensuring fast loading times and an exceptional user experience.

- **Scalability**: Set expectations for scalability. Custom themes can accommodate future design changes and expansion without constraints imposed by pre-built templates.

- **Exclusivity**: Enjoy exclusivity with a custom design. Your theme won't be used by other websites, preventing brand dilution.

Complexities and Challenges of Custom Themes

- **Development Time**: Setting realistic expectations about development time is vital. Custom themes require a longer development period compared to pre-built themes. Plan for thorough design, development, and testing phases.

- **Cost**: Custom themes often come with a higher initial cost due to the extensive design and development involved. Ensure that your budget aligns with the investment required for a custom theme.

- **Maintenance**: Understand that custom themes may require ongoing maintenance, especially after CMS or plugin updates. Setting expectations for maintenance ensures the continued functionality of your theme.

2. Premium Themes

Setting Expectations for Premium Themes

Premium themes are pre-designed templates available for purchase. Setting realistic expectations about premium themes involves understanding their advantages and limitations:

Advantages of Premium Themes

- **Cost-Efficiency**: Premium themes offer cost savings in design and development. They are typically more affordable than custom themes.

- **Quick Deployment**: Expect quick deployment with premium themes. They are ready-made and can be installed and configured promptly.

- **Feature Sets**: Premium themes often come with a range of built-in features, including responsive design, SEO optimization, and customization options.

- **Community and Support**: Many premium themes have active user communities and dedicated support, providing assistance when needed.

- **Updates**: Premium themes receive updates from developers, ensuring compatibility with the latest CMS versions and security patches.

Limitations of Premium Themes

- **Lack of Uniqueness**: Understand that premium themes are widely available, so your design may not be entirely unique. Customization can mitigate this limitation.

- **Feature Restrictions**: Premium themes may have limitations in terms of unique functionality. Consider whether the theme meets your specific feature requirements.

- **Customization Complexity**: Customizing a premium theme extensively may require technical expertise, leading to additional costs or complexity.

- **Scalability**: Ensure that the chosen premium theme can accommodate future design changes or expansion as your portal grows.

- **Updates and Compatibility**: Expect occasional updates to maintain theme compatibility. Setting expectations for these updates ensures continued functionality.

3. Finding the Right Balance

Setting realistic expectations about the balance between custom and premium themes is essential. Consider your budget, design requirements, timeline, and long-term vision for your news portal. Some portals opt for a hybrid approach, using a premium theme as a starting point and customizing it to achieve a unique look and functionality.

In summary, selecting between custom and premium themes involves setting realistic expectations about advantages, complexities, and costs. Your choice should align with your portal's branding, design needs, and budgetary constraints.

Section 5.3: Theme Customization

Customizing your chosen theme is a crucial step in tailoring your news portal's design to your specific needs. This section delves into the various aspects of theme customization:

1. Understanding Theme Customization

Setting realistic expectations about theme customization is essential. Theme customization involves modifying the appearance, layout, and functionality of your chosen theme to align with your news portal's branding and content presentation.

2. Customization Options

Setting Expectations for Customization Options

Evaluate the customization options offered by your theme, which may include:

Design Customization

- **Color Schemes**: Understand the theme's flexibility in choosing color schemes. You should be able to match your branding colors and create a visually cohesive portal.

- **Typography**: Expect options for selecting fonts and font sizes to ensure readability and branding consistency.

- **Layouts**: Assess the theme's layout options, such as single-column, multi-column, or grid layouts. Set expectations for layout flexibility based on your content presentation.

- **Header and Footer Customization**: Ensure that you can customize the header and footer to include elements like logos, navigation menus, and social media links.

Content Customization

- **Post Templates**: Understand if the theme offers various post templates, allowing you to present different types of content uniquely. This is especially important for news articles, opinion pieces, and multimedia content.

- **Featured Content**: Set expectations for featuring specific content prominently, such as top stories, breaking news, or editorials.

- **Widgets and Blocks**: Assess the availability of widgets and content blocks that enable you to add diverse content elements, including advertisements, related articles, and multimedia.

Functionality Customization

- **Plugin Compatibility**: Ensure that the theme is compatible with essential plugins. Set expectations for integrating plugins that enhance functionality, such as SEO tools, social media sharing, and analytics.

- **Custom Menus**: Expect the ability to create custom navigation menus to improve user navigation and categorize content effectively.

- **Mobile Responsiveness**: Confirm that the theme is fully responsive, ensuring that your portal functions seamlessly on various devices and screen sizes.

3. Customization Complexity

Setting realistic expectations about customization complexity is crucial. Depending on your technical skills and familiarity with the chosen theme, customization tasks can range from straightforward changes, like adjusting colors and fonts, to more complex modifications, such as altering layout structures or adding custom code.

4. Visual Editors and Page Builders

If your chosen theme includes visual editors or page builders, setting expectations for their capabilities is important. These tools simplify customization by offering a user-friendly interface for adjusting layouts and adding content elements.

5. Testing and Preview

Before applying customizations to your live portal, setting expectations for testing and previewing is essential. Ensure that you can preview changes in a staging environment to assess their impact on design and functionality.

6. Documentation and Support

Assess the availability of documentation and support resources provided by the theme developer. Comprehensive documentation and support channels can assist you in understanding customization options and addressing any challenges.

7. Backup and Restore

Set expectations for backup and restore procedures. Before making significant customizations, regularly back up your portal to ensure that you can revert to a previous state if issues arise during customization.

8. User Training

If you have a team of contributors and editors, consider providing training to ensure that they can effectively use customization options to create and publish content.

9. Ongoing Customization

Recognize that customization is an ongoing process. As your news portal evolves and user feedback accumulates, you may need to adjust your theme customization to meet changing needs and preferences.

In summary, setting realistic expectations for theme customization involves understanding the available customization options, assessing complexity, and preparing for testing, documentation, and ongoing adjustments. Theme customization allows you to craft a unique and user-friendly design for your news portal.

Section 6.4: Using a Mobile-Friendly Theme or Script - Advantages

In today's digital landscape, the mobile-friendliness of your news portal can significantly impact its success. Let's explore the advantages of using a mobile-friendly theme or script for your news portal.

Advantages of Using a Mobile-Friendly Theme or Script

1. **Improved User Experience**: A mobile-friendly theme or script ensures that your news portal looks and functions well on smartphones and tablets. This leads to a better user experience, reducing bounce rates and increasing engagement.

2. **Expanded Audience Reach**: With mobile-friendliness, your portal becomes accessible to a

broader audience, including users who primarily access the internet through mobile devices. This can lead to increased traffic and readership.

3. **Search Engine Optimization (SEO)**: Mobile-friendliness is a ranking factor in search engines like Google. A responsive or mobile-optimized theme can improve your portal's search engine rankings, resulting in more organic traffic.

4. **Faster Loading Times**: Mobile-friendly themes are often designed for efficient loading on mobile connections, ensuring that your content loads quickly even on slower networks.

5. **Adaptability to Different Devices**: Mobile-friendly themes and scripts are designed to adapt to various screen sizes and resolutions, providing a consistent and visually pleasing experience across devices.

6. **Reduced Maintenance**: Managing a single responsive theme is more straightforward than maintaining separate desktop and mobile versions of your portal. This can save time and resources.

By embracing a mobile-friendly theme or script, your news portal can cater to the growing mobile audience, enhance user experience, and improve search engine rankings.

Setting Expectations for Mobile-Friendly Themes

When considering the adoption of a mobile-friendly theme or script, it's essential to set clear expectations to understand how they can benefit your news portal.

1. **Design Consistency**: Expect your mobile-friendly theme to maintain a consistent design with your desktop version, ensuring brand continuity.

2. **Responsive Design**: Your theme should adapt to different screen sizes seamlessly, from smartphones to tablets.

3. **Optimized Images**: Images should be automatically resized and optimized for mobile devices to reduce loading times.

4. **User-Friendly Navigation**: Mobile themes should offer intuitive navigation with easy access to categories, articles, and multimedia content.

5. **Fast Loading**: Set expectations for fast-loading pages to prevent user frustration and improve SEO.

6. **Compatibility**: Ensure that your chosen theme is compatible with popular browsers and mobile devices.

Understanding these expectations will help you choose the right mobile-friendly theme or script and maximize its benefits for your news portal.

Section 6.5: Generating and Using Applications for Mobile Devices

In today's mobile-centric world, having a dedicated mobile application for your news portal can offer unique benefits. This section explores the process of generating and using mobile applications for mobile devices:

Creating a Mobile Application

1. **Platform Selection**: Decide whether you want to create native apps for specific platforms like iOS and Android or opt for a cross-platform solution like React Native or Flutter.

2. **Development**: Choose whether to develop the app in-house or hire a development team. Ensure the app aligns with your news portal's branding and features.

3. **User Interface (UI) and User Experience (UX)**: Craft an intuitive and visually appealing UI/UX design that makes navigation and content consumption seamless for mobile users.

4. **Content Integration**: Ensure the app integrates smoothly with your news portal's content management system (CMS) to deliver real-time news updates.

Benefits of Having a Mobile App

1. **Enhanced User Engagement**: Mobile apps provide a direct channel to engage with your audience

through push notifications, personalized content, and interactive features.

2. **Offline Access**: Users can access your news content even without an internet connection, making your portal's content available anytime, anywhere.

3. **Brand Loyalty**: A dedicated app fosters brand loyalty, as users are more likely to return to your portal through the app.

4. **Monetization Opportunities**: Apps offer various monetization options, such as in-app advertising, subscriptions, and premium content access.

Section 6.6: Integrating Your Web Portal and Domain with Search Engines

To ensure your news portal is discoverable by a wider audience, it's crucial to integrate it with search engines effectively. This section delves into the process of integrating your web portal and domain with search engines:

Steps for Integration

1. **Submit Sitemaps**: Create and submit XML sitemaps to major search engines like Google and Bing. Sitemaps help search engine bots index your content efficiently.

2. **Robots.txt File**: Customize your website's robots.txt file to instruct search engine crawlers on which pages to crawl and index.

3. **Meta Tags**: Implement meta tags, including title tags and meta descriptions, to optimize how your content appears in search engine results pages (SERPs).

4. **Mobile Optimization**: Ensure your portal is mobile-optimized to cater to mobile users, as search engines prioritize mobile-friendly websites in mobile search results.

5. **Schema Markup**: Implement schema markup to provide search engines with structured data about your content, enabling rich search results, such as featured snippets.

6. **Quality Content**: Continuously publish high-quality, original content that aligns with reader interests and search engine guidelines.

7. **Backlink Building**: Develop a backlink strategy to acquire authoritative and relevant backlinks to your news articles.

Benefits of Integration

1. **Increased Visibility**: Integration with search engines ensures that your news articles are more likely to appear in search results, driving organic traffic.

2. **Better Rankings**: Effective integration practices can improve your portal's search engine rankings, making it more competitive in search results.

3. **Discoverability**: Your news portal becomes easily discoverable by users seeking information on relevant topics, broadening your readership.

4. **Credibility**: High rankings in search results can enhance your portal's credibility and reputation as a reliable news source.

5. **Traffic Growth**: Integration with search engines can lead to consistent and sustainable growth in website traffic, essential for a news portal's success.

By optimizing your news portal for search engines and ensuring mobile-friendliness, you can enhance its discoverability, reach a broader audience, and provide an excellent user experience for both desktop and mobile users.

Chapter 6: Essential Plugins

Section 6.1: Must-Have WordPress Plugins

WordPress plugins are essential tools that enhance the functionality and features of your news portal. This section delves into the must-have plugins for a WordPress-based news website:

1. Setting Expectations for WordPress Plugins

Setting realistic expectations about WordPress plugins involves understanding their role in extending the capabilities of your news portal. Plugins are pieces of software that can add features, functionality, and tools to your WordPress website.

2. SEO Optimization Tools

Setting Expectations for SEO Optimization Tools

Search Engine Optimization (SEO) is critical for driving organic traffic to your news portal. Setting realistic expectations about SEO plugins involves understanding their advantages and considerations:

Advantages of SEO Optimization Tools

- **Improved Visibility**: Expect SEO plugins to provide features for optimizing content, meta tags, and images to improve your portal's search engine rankings.

- **XML Sitemaps**: Look for plugins that generate XML sitemaps, making it easier for search engines to index your content.

- **Keyword Analysis**: Some SEO plugins offer keyword analysis tools to help you choose effective keywords and optimize your content accordingly.

- **SEO Audits**: Set expectations for SEO audits that identify areas for improvement and provide recommendations to enhance your portal's SEO performance.

- **Schema Markup**: Some plugins support schema markup, which enhances the appearance of your content in search engine results with rich snippets.

Considerations for SEO Optimization Tools

- **Learning Curve**: Understand that SEO optimization tools may have a learning curve. Plan to invest time in learning how to use these plugins effectively.

- **Regular Updates**: Set expectations for regular updates to ensure that your chosen SEO plugin remains compatible with the latest WordPress versions and search engine algorithms.

- **Compatibility**: Ensure that the SEO plugin is compatible with your chosen theme and other plugins. Compatibility issues can affect your website's performance.

3. Performance and Caching Plugins

Setting Expectations for Performance and Caching Plugins

Performance optimization is crucial for fast loading times and a smooth user experience. Setting realistic expectations about performance and caching plugins involves understanding their benefits and considerations:

Advantages of Performance and Caching Plugins

- **Caching**: Expect caching plugins to create static versions of your web pages, reducing server load and improving page loading speed.

- **Minification**: Some plugins offer code minification, which reduces the size of CSS, JavaScript, and HTML files for faster loading.

- **Content Delivery Network (CDN) Integration**: Look for plugins that integrate with CDNs to distribute content globally, reducing latency for users in different regions.

- **Image Optimization**: Certain plugins can automatically optimize images, reducing their file size without compromising quality.

- **Database Cleanup**: Expect database optimization features to remove unnecessary data and improve website performance.

Considerations for Performance and Caching Plugins

- **Compatibility**: Ensure that the chosen performance plugin works well with your theme and other plugins. Compatibility issues can affect your website's functionality.

- **Configuration**: Understand that performance optimization often requires fine-tuning settings. Set aside time to configure the plugin according to your portal's needs.

- **Regular Maintenance**: Performance plugins may require periodic monitoring and adjustment to maintain optimal speed and functionality.

4. Security Plugins

Setting Expectations for Security Plugins

Security is paramount for protecting your news portal and user data. Setting realistic expectations about security plugins involves understanding their advantages and considerations:

Advantages of Security Plugins

- **Firewalls**: Expect security plugins to provide firewall protection against malicious attacks, including hacking attempts and DDoS attacks.

- **Malware Scanning**: Look for plugins that offer malware scanning and removal capabilities to keep your portal free from harmful code.

- **Login Security**: Some security plugins offer login attempt monitoring, two-factor authentication (2FA), and login lockdown features to prevent unauthorized access.

- **Security Audits**: Set expectations for security audits that identify vulnerabilities and provide recommendations for strengthening your portal's security.

Considerations for Security Plugins

- **Regular Updates**: Security plugins should receive regular updates to protect against emerging threats. Set expectations for timely updates and compatibility with the latest WordPress versions.

- **False Positives**: Understand that security scans may sometimes produce false positives. It's important to review scan results carefully and take appropriate action.

- **Backup and Restore**: Some security plugins offer backup and restore features. Ensure that you have a backup strategy in place to safeguard your portal's data.

5. User Experience Enhancement Plugins

Setting Expectations for User Experience Enhancement Plugins

User experience is vital for retaining and engaging readers. Setting realistic expectations about user experience enhancement plugins involves understanding their benefits and considerations:

Advantages of User Experience Enhancement Plugins

- **Content Display**: Expect plugins that enhance content display with features like related articles, popular posts, and featured content sections.

- **Social Sharing**: Look for plugins that facilitate social media sharing, making it easy for readers to share your articles on various platforms.

- **Comment Management**: Some plugins offer advanced comment management tools, including spam protection and moderation features.

- **Newsletter Integration**: Consider plugins that integrate with newsletter services to capture reader email addresses and build your subscriber list.

Considerations for User Experience Enhancement Plugins

- **Compatibility**: Ensure that the chosen plugins are compatible with your theme and other website elements to avoid conflicts.

- **Performance Impact**: Some feature-rich plugins may have a performance impact. Evaluate the performance of your portal after plugin installation.

- **Customization**: Set expectations for customization options to tailor the appearance and behavior of these plugins to your portal's design and user preferences.

6. Analytics and Tracking Plugins

Setting Expectations for Analytics and Tracking Plugins

Analytics tools provide insights into your portal's performance and audience behavior. Setting realistic expectations about analytics and tracking plugins involves understanding their advantages and considerations:

Advantages of Analytics and Tracking Plugins

- **Audience Insights**: Expect plugins to provide valuable audience data, including page views, user demographics, and referral sources.

- **Conversion Tracking**: Some plugins offer conversion tracking to monitor specific user actions, such as sign-ups or subscriptions.

- **Content Performance**: Analyze the performance of your articles and content types to identify what resonates with your audience.

- **A/B Testing**: Certain plugins enable A/B testing of headlines, images, and other elements to optimize user engagement.

- **Integration**: Look for plugins that integrate with popular analytics platforms like Google Analytics for comprehensive data collection.

Considerations for Analytics and Tracking Plugins

- **Privacy Compliance**: Ensure that your tracking practices align with privacy regulations like GDPR. Inform users about data collection and use through clear privacy policies.

- **Data Accuracy**: Regularly review and validate analytics data for accuracy. Understand that data interpretation may require expertise.

- **Reporting**: Set expectations for reporting features to generate actionable insights from the data collected.

In summary, setting realistic expectations about essential WordPress plugins involves understanding their roles, advantages, considerations, and potential impact on your news portal's functionality. Careful selection and configuration of plugins can significantly enhance your portal's performance, security, user experience, and analytics capabilities.

Section 6.2: SEO Optimization Tools

Search Engine Optimization (SEO) is a cornerstone of news portal success. This section explores the essential SEO optimization tools and strategies for enhancing your portal's visibility in search engine results:

1. Setting Expectations for SEO Optimization Tools

Setting realistic expectations about SEO optimization tools is crucial for understanding how they can impact your news portal's reach and audience engagement. SEO tools are designed to help you optimize your website for search engines like Google, making it easier for users to discover your content.

2. On-Page SEO

Setting Expectations for On-Page SEO

On-page SEO involves optimizing individual web pages to improve their search engine rankings. Setting realistic expectations for on-page SEO involves understanding its components and benefits:

Components of On-Page SEO

- **Keyword Research**: Expect to perform in-depth keyword research to identify relevant and high-traffic keywords related to your news articles. Tools like Google Keyword Planner and SEMrush can assist in this process.

- **Content Optimization**: Set expectations for optimizing your news articles with selected keywords. This includes strategically placing keywords in titles, headings, meta descriptions, and throughout the content.

- **Quality Content**: Understand that high-quality, informative, and engaging content is paramount for on-page SEO. Ensure that your articles provide value to readers.

- **Image Optimization**: Expect to optimize images by using descriptive file names and alt tags. This improves accessibility and search engine indexing.

- **Internal Linking**: Internal linking, where you link to other relevant articles within your portal, aids in user navigation and helps search engines understand the structure of your website.

Benefits of On-Page SEO

- **Improved Rankings**: Proper on-page optimization can lead to higher search engine rankings for your news articles, increasing their visibility to users.

- **Better User Experience**: Optimized content is user-friendly, providing a seamless reading experience that keeps visitors on your website longer.

- **Higher Click-Through Rates**: When your articles appear in search results with compelling titles and descriptions, users are more likely to click through to your portal.

3. Technical SEO

Setting Expectations for Technical SEO

Technical SEO focuses on the behind-the-scenes elements that impact your website's performance in search engines. Setting realistic expectations for technical SEO involves understanding its components and significance:

Components of Technical SEO

- **Site Speed**: Expect to optimize your website for fast loading times. Slow-loading websites can result in higher bounce rates and lower search engine rankings.

- **Mobile Optimization**: Set expectations for mobile responsiveness. With a growing number of users accessing news on mobile devices, mobile optimization is critical for SEO.

- **Crawlability**: Ensure that search engine bots can crawl and index your website effectively. Resolve any issues that may hinder crawling, such as broken links or inaccessible pages.

- **Structured Data Markup**: Understand the concept of structured data markup, which allows you to provide additional information to search engines about the content on your portal, potentially leading to rich search results.

- **XML Sitemaps**: Expect to generate and submit XML sitemaps to search engines to help them understand your website's structure and content hierarchy.

Benefits of Technical SEO

- **Improved User Experience**: Technical SEO enhancements, such as fast loading times and mobile optimization, contribute to a better user experience.

- **Enhanced Indexing**: When search engines can crawl and index your website efficiently, your news articles are more likely to appear in search results.

- **Reduced Bounce Rate**: A well-optimized website is less likely to have a high bounce rate, which can negatively impact search engine rankings.

4. Off-Page SEO

Setting Expectations for Off-Page SEO

Off-page SEO focuses on external factors that can influence your news portal's search engine rankings. Setting realistic expectations for off-page SEO involves understanding its components and potential impact:

Components of Off-Page SEO

- **Backlink Building**: Expect to engage in backlink building efforts to acquire high-quality, authoritative links from other websites. Quality backlinks are a significant ranking factor.

- **Social Signals**: Understand the role of social signals in off-page SEO. Social media engagement, shares, and mentions can indirectly impact search engine rankings.

- **Online Reputation Management**: Set expectations for monitoring and managing your news portal's online reputation. Negative reviews or mentions can affect your credibility.

- **Guest Posting**: Consider guest posting on reputable websites to build authority and acquire backlinks. However, set expectations for quality over quantity in your guest posting efforts.

Benefits of Off-Page SEO

- **Increased Authority**: Off-page SEO efforts can establish your portal as an authoritative source of news, leading to improved search engine rankings.

- **Expanded Reach**: High-quality backlinks and social signals can extend your portal's reach, driving more traffic and engagement.

- **Trust and Credibility**: An online reputation management strategy ensures that your news portal is viewed as trustworthy and credible by readers and search engines alike.

Setting realistic expectations for SEO optimization tools and strategies involves recognizing the multifaceted nature of SEO. While on-page, technical, and off-page SEO are essential components, it's crucial to prioritize quality content and user experience as the foundation of your news portal's success.

Section 6.3: Enhancing User Experience

User experience (UX) is a pivotal aspect of retaining readers and building a loyal audience for your news portal. This section explores the essential plugins and strategies for enhancing user experience:

1. Setting Expectations for Enhancing User Experience

Setting realistic expectations about enhancing user experience involves understanding how plugins and strategies can contribute to making your news portal more engaging, user-friendly, and valuable to readers.

2. Content Display Plugins

Setting Expectations for Content Display Plugins

Content display plugins play a crucial role in presenting your news articles and multimedia content in an appealing and user-friendly manner. Setting realistic expectations for content display plugins involves understanding their features and benefits:

Features of Content Display Plugins

- **Responsive Design**: Expect plugins to provide responsive design elements that ensure your content looks great on various devices and screen sizes.

- **Custom Templates**: Some plugins offer customizable templates for presenting different types of content, such as news articles, opinion pieces, or multimedia features.

- **Featured Content**: Look for features that allow you to highlight and feature specific articles or content on your homepage or category pages.

- **Infinite Scroll**: Some plugins offer infinite scroll functionality, allowing readers to seamlessly navigate through your content without having to load new pages.

Benefits of Content Display Plugins

- **Improved Readability**: Content display plugins enhance the readability of your articles, ensuring that readers can easily consume your news.

- **Engaging Multimedia**: Features like image sliders, galleries, and embedded videos can make your articles more engaging and visually appealing.

- **Efficient Navigation**: Plugins with features like related articles and category filters improve navigation, helping readers discover more content.

3. Social Sharing and Engagement Plugins

Setting Expectations for Social Sharing and Engagement Plugins

Social sharing and engagement plugins empower readers to interact with your content and share it on social media. Setting realistic expectations for these plugins involves understanding their role in increasing your portal's visibility and audience engagement:

Features of Social Sharing and Engagement Plugins

- **Share Buttons**: Expect share buttons for popular social media platforms like Facebook, Twitter, and LinkedIn, making it easy for readers to share your articles.

- **Comment Systems**: Look for plugins that offer robust comment systems with features like threaded discussions, moderation tools, and spam protection.

- **Like and Share Counts**: Some plugins display like and share counts, showcasing the popularity of your articles and encouraging further engagement.

- **Social Login**: Consider plugins that allow readers to log in or comment using their social media profiles, reducing friction for engagement.

Benefits of Social Sharing and Engagement Plugins

- **Wider Reach**: Social sharing buttons enable readers to amplify your content by sharing it with their social networks, potentially reaching a broader audience.

- **Community Building**: Robust comment systems foster a sense of community around your news portal, encouraging readers to engage in discussions.

- **User Feedback**: Comments and likes provide valuable feedback on your articles, allowing you to gauge reader sentiment and preferences.

4. Newsletter Subscription and Notification Plugins

Setting Expectations for Newsletter Subscription and Notification Plugins

Newsletter plugins are essential for building a subscriber base and keeping readers informed about your latest articles. Setting realistic expectations for these plugins involves understanding their features and benefits:

Features of Newsletter Subscription and Notification Plugins

- **Subscription Forms**: Expect plugins to offer customizable subscription forms that you can place strategically on your portal to capture reader emails.

- **Automated Emails**: Look for plugins that automate email newsletters, sending updates about new articles, special features, or editorials to subscribers.

- **Segmentation**: Some plugins allow you to segment your subscriber list based on reader preferences or interests, enabling targeted content delivery.

- **Notification Bars**: Consider plugins that provide notification bars or pop-ups to promote newsletter sign-ups and special announcements.

Benefits of Newsletter Subscription and Notification Plugins

- **Audience Growth**: Newsletter plugins help you build a subscriber base, allowing you to reach readers directly in their inboxes.

- **Engagement Retention**: Regular newsletter updates keep readers engaged and informed, encouraging them to return to your portal for fresh content.

- **Personalization**: Segmentation and targeting options enable you to tailor newsletter content to specific reader interests, increasing relevance and engagement.

5. Analytics and User Tracking Plugins

Setting Expectations for Analytics and User Tracking Plugins

Analytics and user tracking plugins provide valuable insights into user behavior on your news portal. Setting realistic expectations for these plugins involves understanding how they can help you optimize your portal for user engagement:

Features of Analytics and User Tracking Plugins

- **Audience Insights**: Expect plugins to offer audience demographic data, behavior patterns, and pageview statistics to help you understand your readers.

- **Conversion Tracking**: Some plugins provide conversion tracking, allowing you to monitor specific actions users take, such as signing up for newsletters or subscribing.

- **Content Performance**: Look for features that analyze the performance of individual articles, helping you identify which topics resonate most with your audience.

- **A/B Testing**: Certain plugins enable A/B testing of headlines, images, or content elements to optimize user engagement.

Benefits of Analytics and User Tracking Plugins

- **Informed Decision-Making**: Analytics data guides your editorial and content strategy by revealing what content is popular and where user engagement can be improved.

- **User-Centric Improvements**: Tracking user behavior helps you make user-centric improvements to your portal, enhancing the overall experience.

- **Goal Achievement**: Conversion tracking allows you to measure the success of specific goals, such as increasing subscriptions or ad clicks.

Enhancing user experience through plugins involves selecting the right tools to streamline content display, encourage engagement, and provide valuable insights. By setting clear expectations and maximizing the benefits of these plugins, your news portal can create a satisfying and memorable experience for your readers.

Chapter 7: Partnering with News Agencies

Section 7.1: Establishing Relationships

Partnering with news agencies is a strategic move that can enhance the content and credibility of your news portal. In this section, we will explore the vital steps involved in establishing fruitful relationships with news agencies:

1. Identifying Potential News Agency Partners

Before you can establish partnerships, it's crucial to identify potential news agencies that align with your portal's niche and target audience. Consider the following when seeking partners:

- **Relevance**: Look for agencies that cover topics related to your news portal's focus, ensuring a natural synergy.

- **Credibility**: Prioritize agencies with a strong reputation for accurate and reliable reporting.

- **Content Quality**: Evaluate the quality of their content to ensure it meets your editorial standards.

- **Audience Reach**: Assess the reach of potential partners to gauge the potential impact on your portal's readership.

2. Building Initial Contact

Once you've identified prospective partners, the next step is to establish initial contact. Approach this step professionally:

- **Introduction**: Send a well-crafted email introducing your news portal, its mission, and the potential benefits of collaboration.

- **Personalization**: Tailor your messages to each agency to demonstrate your genuine interest in their work.

- **Clear Intentions**: Be transparent about your intentions to explore partnership opportunities and mutual benefits.

3. Building Trust and Rapport

Successful partnerships are built on trust and rapport. Here's how to foster these qualities:

- **Transparency**: Maintain open and honest communication throughout the negotiation process.

- **Reliability**: Deliver on promises and deadlines to establish your portal's reliability.

- **Face-to-Face Meetings**: Whenever possible, arrange face-to-face meetings or video conferences to build a stronger connection.

4. Collaborative Agreements

Once initial discussions are fruitful, it's time to formalize the partnership with collaborative agreements:

- **Content Sharing**: Define the terms of content sharing, including the frequency, types of content, and attribution.

- **Legal Considerations**: Consult legal experts to ensure that agreements comply with copyright and intellectual property laws.

- **Mutual Goals**: Establish mutual goals and expectations for the partnership's success.

5. Content Integration

With agreements in place, begin integrating the content of your news agency partners into your portal:

- **Integration Tools**: Utilize content management systems (CMS) or APIs to seamlessly incorporate partner content.

- **Attribution**: Clearly attribute partner content to maintain transparency and give credit where it's due.

- **Consistency**: Ensure that the integration process aligns with your portal's design and style.

6. Monitoring and Evaluation

Regularly monitor the performance of the partnership:

- **KPIs**: Define key performance indicators (KPIs) to track the partnership's impact on traffic, engagement, and readership.

- **Feedback**: Seek feedback from both your audience and news agency partners to identify areas for improvement.

- **Adaptation**: Be prepared to adapt and refine the partnership based on ongoing evaluations.

7. Long-Term Relationship Building

Building long-term relationships with news agencies is the ultimate goal. Maintain the relationship through:

- **Regular Updates**: Keep partners informed about your portal's growth, achievements, and new initiatives.

- **Collaborative Projects**: Explore opportunities for joint projects, special features, or investigative reporting.

- **Mutual Promotion**: Collaborate on promotional efforts to increase each other's visibility and reach.

By following these steps and nurturing strong relationships, your news portal can establish meaningful partnerships with news agencies, enriching your content and providing valuable insights to your readers.

Section 7.2: Content Syndication Agreements

Content syndication is a powerful strategy that allows news portals to access a broader range of content and reach a wider audience. In this section, we will explore the key elements of content syndication agreements:

1. Understanding Content Syndication

Content syndication involves the distribution and publication of news articles, features, or multimedia content produced by news agencies on your news portal. This partnership allows you to expand your content offerings and provide readers with a more diverse range of news.

2. Identifying Suitable Content

Before entering into content syndication agreements, it's essential to identify the types of content that align with your portal's niche and audience. Consider the following factors when selecting content:

- **Relevance**: Ensure that syndicated content complements your portal's focus and editorial style.

- **Quality**: Assess the quality and accuracy of the content to maintain your portal's credibility.

- **Audience Appeal**: Evaluate whether the content resonates with your target audience and addresses their interests.

3. Negotiating Syndication Terms

Successful content syndication partnerships rely on clear and mutually beneficial terms:

- **Licensing**: Determine the licensing terms for syndicated content. Common options include exclusive, non-exclusive, or limited licenses.

- **Attribution**: Define how syndicated content will be attributed to the source agency, including proper bylines and credits.

- **Content Selection**: Specify the frequency and selection process for syndicated content to ensure a steady flow of relevant articles.

- **Monetary Agreements**: Discuss any financial arrangements, such as revenue-sharing models or flat fees for syndicated content.

4. Legal Considerations

Content syndication agreements should comply with legal and copyright regulations:

- **Intellectual Property Rights**: Ensure that you have the legal right to syndicate the content and that the source agency holds the necessary intellectual property rights.

- **Permissions**: Verify that you have obtained explicit permission to use and display the syndicated content on your portal.

- **Exclusivity**: Clarify whether syndication agreements grant exclusive rights to the content or allow the source agency to syndicate it to other platforms simultaneously.

5. Integration and Presentation

Once content syndication agreements are in place, it's time to seamlessly integrate syndicated content into your news portal:

- **Integration Tools**: Utilize content management systems (CMS) or APIs to automate the integration process and ensure the timely publication of syndicated articles.

- **Stylistic Consistency**: Maintain a consistent look and feel for syndicated content in terms of formatting, fonts, and design.

- **Editorial Oversight**: Implement a review process to ensure that syndicated content aligns with your portal's editorial guidelines.

6. Performance Monitoring

Regularly monitor the performance of syndicated content:

- **Engagement Metrics**: Track engagement metrics such as pageviews, shares, and comments to assess the impact of syndicated articles on your portal's readership.

- **Quality Assessment**: Continuously evaluate the quality and relevance of syndicated content to maintain a high editorial standard.

- **Feedback Loop**: Establish a feedback loop with source agencies to address any concerns or improvements related to content syndication.

7. Maintaining Editorial Independence

While syndicating content can enrich your portal, it's essential to maintain editorial independence:

- **Editorial Guidelines**: Clearly communicate your editorial guidelines to source agencies to ensure that syndicated content aligns with your portal's mission and values.

- **Editing Rights**: Define the extent to which you can edit or adapt syndicated content to maintain consistency with your portal's style.

By carefully navigating content syndication agreements and adhering to ethical and legal standards, your news portal can leverage the benefits of syndicated content while preserving its editorial integrity.

Section 7.3: Copyright and Fair Use

Copyright laws play a pivotal role in content syndication and publishing. This section will explore the essential considerations related to copyright and fair use when partnering with news agencies:

1. Understanding Copyright

Copyright is a legal framework that grants creators and content producers exclusive rights to their work. When partnering with news agencies, it's crucial to respect copyright laws:

- **Ownership**: Understand that news agencies typically hold the copyright to the content they produce, including articles, images, and videos.

- **Duration**: Copyright protection lasts for a specific duration, typically the creator's lifetime plus 70 years. Be aware of the copyright status of any content you wish to syndicate.

2. Licensing and Permission

To legally syndicate content, you must obtain the necessary licensing or permissions:

- **Explicit Consent**: Seek explicit consent from news agencies to syndicate their content. This consent is usually documented in content syndication agreements.

- **License Terms**: Ensure that syndication agreements specify the scope of the license, including usage rights, attribution requirements, and any associated fees.

3. Fair Use Doctrine

Fair use is a doctrine within copyright law that allows for the limited use of copyrighted material without the need for permission or payment under specific circumstances. Key considerations include:

- **Purpose**: Fair use typically applies when content is used for purposes such as commentary, criticism, news reporting, or educational use.

- **Nature of the Work**: Consider whether the content is factual or creative. Fair use is more likely to apply to factual information.

- **Amount Used**: The extent to which copyrighted material is used matters. Using small portions or excerpts is more likely to be considered fair use.

- **Effect on Market**: Assess whether your use of the content could negatively impact the market value of the original work. Avoid using content in a way that could harm its commercial value.

4. Public Domain and Creative Commons

Content that is in the public domain or released under Creative Commons licenses can be used more freely:

- **Public Domain**: Works in the public domain are not protected by copyright and can be used without restrictions. Ensure that you verify the public domain status of any content you plan to use.

- **Creative Commons**: Content released under Creative Commons licenses often allows for various levels of use, provided you adhere to the terms specified in the license (e.g., attribution, non-commercial use).

5. Proper Attribution

Proper attribution is essential when using copyrighted material:

- **Clear Attribution**: Clearly attribute the source of syndicated content, following any guidelines set in syndication agreements.

- **Bylines and Credits**: Respect the bylines and credits of original creators and agencies to acknowledge their work.

6. Legal Consultation

When in doubt regarding copyright matters, consider seeking legal consultation:

- **Legal Expertise**: Engage legal experts who specialize in copyright law to ensure that your syndication practices comply with legal standards.

- **Risk Mitigation**: Legal consultation can help you assess and mitigate potential legal risks associated with content syndication.

By understanding copyright laws, securing proper permissions, and adhering to fair use principles, your news portal can navigate content syndication ethically and legally, enhancing your content offerings while respecting the rights of content creators and agencies.

Chapter 8: Building Popularity and Readership

Section 8.1: Content Strategy and Quality - The Foundation of Success

Understanding the Crucial Role of Content Strategy

A well-defined content strategy is the compass that guides your news portal's journey. It's more than just planning what to publish; it's a comprehensive approach to content creation, distribution, and management. Here's an in-depth look at the components of a successful content strategy:

1. Audience Segmentation - Know Your Readers

Before crafting content, you must understand your readers inside out. Audience segmentation involves breaking down your readership into distinct groups based on demographics, behavior, and interests. By doing so, you can tailor your content to meet the specific needs and preferences of each segment. This personalized approach enhances reader engagement and loyalty.

2. Content Goals - Setting Clear Objectives

Every piece of content should have a purpose. Whether it's to inform, entertain, or inspire, setting clear objectives for your content is essential. These goals might include increasing website traffic, boosting social media engagement, or driving revenue through advertising. Having defined content goals helps you measure success and track progress effectively.

3. Editorial Calendar - The Backbone of Consistency

An editorial calendar is your roadmap for content creation and publication. It outlines what content will be produced, when it will be published, and who is responsible for creating it. A well-structured editorial calendar ensures that your news portal consistently delivers fresh and relevant content, keeping your readers engaged.

4. Keyword Research - Unlocking SEO Potential

Keyword research is a fundamental aspect of content strategy, especially in the digital age. By identifying the keywords and phrases that are relevant to your niche, you can optimize your content for search engines. This means your articles are more likely to appear in search results, attracting organic traffic and expanding your readership.

The Quest for Quality Content

High-quality content is not just a preference; it's a necessity. It's what sets your news portal apart and establishes trust with your audience. Let's delve deeper into the elements of quality content:

1. Accuracy and Credibility - The Pillars of Trust

In the news industry, trust is paramount. Readers turn to your portal for reliable information. Accuracy and credibility are non-negotiable. You must fact-check rigorously, attribute sources transparently, and maintain a commitment to truthful reporting. Building and preserving trust is a long-term investment.

2. Relevance - Staying Aligned with Audience Interests

Relevance is a dynamic quality. Your content must stay aligned with current events, trends, and your audience's interests. This requires continuous monitoring of news cycles and audience behavior. Tailoring your content to what matters most to your readers keeps them engaged and returning for more.

3. Engagement - Fostering Reader Interaction

Quality content should not be a one-way street. It should encourage reader interaction. Engaging content invites comments, shares, and discussions. It sparks curiosity and prompts readers to voice their opinions. Creating this sense of community around your portal strengthens reader loyalty.

4. Multimedia Integration - Enhancing the Reading Experience

Today's readers expect more than text alone. High-quality content often incorporates multimedia elements such as images, videos, infographics, and interactive features. These elements not only make content more engaging but also aid in conveying complex information effectively.

5. Grammar and Style - The Craft of Professionalism

Consistency in grammar, style, and formatting is a hallmark of professionalism. Errors in these areas can erode trust and credibility. A meticulous approach to editing and adherence to your portal's established style guide are vital.

Maintaining Ethical Integrity

Lastly, maintaining ethical integrity is at the core of quality content. This includes practicing objective and unbiased reporting, respecting copyright and intellectual property rights, and disclosing conflicts of interest when necessary. Upholding these ethical standards builds trust with your readers.

By understanding the intricacies of content strategy and the critical importance of quality content, your news portal can attract and retain a dedicated readership. It's a continuous journey of improvement and adaptation to meet the evolving needs and expectations of your audience.

Section 8.1.1: Content Strategy and Quality

Content is the lifeblood of any news portal, and crafting a well-defined content strategy while maintaining high-quality content is crucial for building popularity and readership. In this section, we will explore the key elements of a successful content strategy and how it relates to content quality:

1. Defining Your Content Strategy

A content strategy serves as the blueprint for creating, publishing, and managing content on your news portal:

- **Audience Segmentation**: Identify and understand your target audience's preferences, interests, and information needs.

- **Content Goals**: Set clear objectives for your content, such as increasing readership, engagement, or revenue generation.

- **Editorial Calendar**: Develop a structured editorial calendar that outlines content topics, publication schedules, and special features.

- **Keyword Research**: Conduct keyword research to optimize your content for search engines and align it with reader queries.

2. Content Quality Standards

High-quality content is the cornerstone of a successful news portal. Consider the following aspects when evaluating content quality:

- **Accuracy and Credibility**: Ensure that news articles are factually accurate and based on reliable sources to maintain trust with your audience.

- **Relevance**: Create content that is relevant to current events, trends, and your audience's interests.

- **Engagement**: Craft content that encourages reader engagement through comments, shares, and discussions.

- **Multimedia Integration**: Enhance articles with multimedia elements such as images, videos, infographics, and interactive features.

- **Grammar and Style**: Maintain consistent grammar, style, and formatting throughout your content to ensure professionalism.

3. Editorial Guidelines

Establish clear editorial guidelines to maintain consistency and uphold editorial standards:

- **Tone and Voice**: Define the tone and voice of your news portal, ensuring that it aligns with your brand identity.

- **Ethical Journalism**: Emphasize ethical journalism practices, including objectivity, fairness, and unbiased reporting.

- **Plagiarism Policies**: Set strict policies against plagiarism and ensure that all content is original or properly attributed.

- **Sourcing**: Clearly outline the process for verifying information sources and attributing them appropriately.

4. Diverse Content Formats

Diversifying content formats can cater to a broader audience and enhance engagement:

- **News Articles**: Deliver timely and informative news articles that cover current events and developments.

- **Opinion Pieces**: Include opinion pieces and editorials that offer diverse perspectives and analysis.

- **Feature Stories**: Craft in-depth feature stories, interviews, and investigative journalism pieces.

- **Multimedia Content**: Create engaging multimedia content, including videos, podcasts, and interactive graphics.

5. Monitoring and Feedback

Regularly monitor content performance and gather feedback to improve:

- **Analytics**: Utilize web analytics tools to track key metrics like pageviews, bounce rates, and user engagement.

- **Reader Feedback**: Encourage reader feedback through comments and surveys to understand their preferences and suggestions.

- **Iterative Improvement**: Continuously iterate on your content strategy based on data and feedback to optimize reader satisfaction.

6. Adaptation to Trends

Stay attuned to industry trends and evolving reader preferences:

- **Emerging Topics**: Be agile in covering emerging topics and trends that matter to your audience.

- **Technology Integration**: Explore innovative technologies, such as AI-driven content recommendations, to enhance user experiences.

- **Audience Expansion**: Consider expanding your audience base by addressing new niches or demographics.

By developing a robust content strategy that emphasizes quality, relevance, and engagement, your news portal can attract and retain a loyal readership. Remember that a strong content strategy is dynamic, evolving alongside industry trends and audience needs.

Section 8.2: Social Media Promotion

Harnessing the Power of Connectivity

In the digital age, social media has emerged as a potent tool for news portals to connect with their audience, amplify their reach, and build a strong online presence. Here, we will explore the intricacies of social media promotion and how it can fuel the growth of your news portal:

1. The Landscape of Social Media

To effectively utilize social media for promotion, it's vital to comprehend the landscape:

- **Platform Selection**: Choose the social media platforms that align with your audience's demographics and interests. Common choices include Facebook, Twitter, Instagram, LinkedIn, and YouTube.

- **Audience Behavior**: Understand how your target audience engages with content on each platform. Some prefer short, snappy updates, while others engage with long-form content.

- **Algorithmic Changes**: Stay informed about algorithmic changes on social media platforms as they can impact the visibility of your content.

2. Crafting Engaging Social Media Content

Creating content that resonates with your social media audience is key:

- **Storytelling**: Leverage the power of storytelling to make your content relatable and emotionally engaging.

- **Visual Appeal**: Visual content, such as images, infographics, and videos, often performs exceptionally well on social media. Invest in high-quality visuals.

- **Consistency**: Maintain a regular posting schedule to keep your audience engaged and informed.

3. Building a Social Media Community

A thriving social media community can be a valuable asset:

- **Engagement**: Respond promptly to comments and messages, fostering a sense of community and demonstrating your commitment to your readers.

- **User-Generated Content**: Encourage readers to contribute their content, such as user reviews or stories, which can enhance your social media presence.

- **Hashtags**: Effectively use hashtags to increase the discoverability of your content.

4. Utilizing Paid Advertising

Paid advertising can amplify your social media reach:

- **Targeted Campaigns**: Create targeted advertising campaigns to reach specific demographics or interests.

- **Measuring ROI**: Use analytics tools to measure the return on investment (ROI) of your paid advertising efforts.

- **A/B Testing**: Continuously refine your paid advertising strategy through A/B testing to optimize results.

5. Analytics and Performance Tracking

Regularly monitor and analyze the performance of your social media efforts:

- **Metrics**: Track key metrics such as engagement rate, reach, click-through rate (CTR), and conversion rate.
- **Audience Insights**: Gain insights into your audience's behavior and preferences through analytics.
- **Competitor Analysis**: Study the social media strategies of competitors to identify opportunities and gaps.

6. Crisis Management

Social media can be a double-edged sword, and managing crises is essential:

- **Preparation**: Have a crisis management plan in place to respond swiftly and effectively to negative incidents or feedback.
- **Transparency**: Maintain transparency in your responses to regain trust during a crisis.
- **Learning from Crises**: Use crises as opportunities to learn and improve your social media strategy.

7. Staying Current with Trends

Social media is constantly evolving, and staying current is critical:

- **Emerging Platforms**: Be open to exploring emerging platforms that may become the next big thing.

- **New Features**: Stay updated on new features and tools offered by existing platforms and incorporate them into your strategy.

- **Content Trends**: Keep an eye on content trends and adapt your approach to meet changing audience preferences.

8. Consistency and Patience

Building a strong social media presence takes time:

- **Consistency**: Stay consistent in your efforts, even if you don't see immediate results.

- **Patience**: Understand that social media promotion is a long-term strategy that requires patience and persistence.

Harnessing the power of social media promotion can significantly boost your news portal's visibility, engagement, and readership. By understanding the intricacies of each social media platform, tailoring your content, and staying agile in response to trends, your news portal can thrive in the digital era.

Section 8.3: SEO and Organic Traffic

The Art of Search Engine Visibility

Unlocking the Potential of SEO for Your News Portal

Search engine optimization (SEO) is a pivotal element of modern digital journalism. It empowers your news portal to gain visibility in search engine results, driving organic traffic. In this section, we will explore the intricacies of SEO and how it can elevate your news portal's online presence:

1. The Foundations of SEO

Understanding the fundamental principles of SEO is crucial:

- **Keyword Research**: Start with comprehensive keyword research to identify the terms and phrases your audience is searching for. Utilize tools like Google Keyword Planner or SEMrush to discover relevant keywords.

- **On-Page SEO**: Optimize on-page elements such as title tags, meta descriptions, headings, and URL structures to align with target keywords.

- **High-Quality Content**: Quality content is at the core of SEO. Craft articles that are informative, engaging, and well-researched, meeting the needs of your audience.

2. Technical SEO

Technical SEO focuses on the behind-the-scenes aspects of your website:

- **Site Speed**: Ensure fast loading times to enhance user experience and meet search engine expectations.

- **Mobile Optimization**: With the increasing use of mobile devices, it's vital to have a mobile-friendly design.

- **Site Structure**: Create a clear and logical site structure, making it easier for search engines to crawl and index your content.

3. Backlink Building

Backlinks, or external links from other websites to yours, are a critical aspect of SEO:

- **Quality over Quantity**: Prioritize high-quality backlinks from reputable sources rather than a large number of low-quality links.

- **Guest Blogging**: Consider guest blogging on other authoritative websites in your niche to build backlinks.

- **Internal Linking**: Utilize internal links within your content to connect related articles and enhance user navigation.

4. Content Strategy and Freshness

Your content strategy plays a significant role in SEO:

- **Evergreen Content**: Create evergreen content that remains relevant over time, attracting consistent traffic.

- **Updating Content**: Regularly update and refresh older articles to ensure accuracy and relevance.

- **Keyword Integration**: Integrate target keywords naturally into your content, avoiding keyword stuffing.

5. Local SEO (if applicable)

For news portals with a local focus, local SEO is crucial:

- **Google My Business**: Set up and optimize your Google My Business listing with accurate information.

- **Local Keywords**: Target local keywords to capture regional audiences.

- **Local Citations**: Ensure consistency in your business's name, address, and phone number (NAP) across online directories.

6. User Experience and Engagement

User experience is a ranking factor in SEO:

- **Mobile Responsiveness**: Ensure your website is fully responsive for mobile users.

- **Page Experience**: Pay attention to Google's Core Web Vitals, which include metrics like page loading speed, interactivity, and visual stability.

- **Engagement Metrics**: High user engagement, such as longer time on site and lower bounce rates, can positively impact SEO.

7. Analytics and Monitoring

Regularly monitor and analyze SEO performance:

- **Web Analytics**: Use tools like Google Analytics to track key metrics such as organic traffic, click-through rates, and user behavior.

- **Search Console**: Leverage Google Search Console to identify and resolve issues that affect your site's visibility.

- **Competitor Analysis**: Study the SEO strategies of competitors to identify opportunities and gaps.

8. Ethical SEO Practices

Maintaining ethical integrity in SEO is essential:

- **Avoid Black Hat Tactics**: Refrain from using black hat SEO techniques such as keyword stuffing, cloaking, or buying backlinks, as these can lead to penalties.

- **Transparency**: Be transparent in your SEO practices, providing clear information to both search engines and users.

- **Algorithm Updates**: Stay updated on search engine algorithm changes to adapt your SEO strategy accordingly.

By mastering the art of SEO, your news portal can gain organic visibility, attract a broader audience, and establish itself as a trusted source of information. It's an ongoing effort that requires dedication, adaptability, and a commitment to providing valuable content.

Chapter 9: Finding Advertisement Revenue

Section 9.1: Advertising Models

Diversifying Your Revenue Streams

Understanding the Landscape of Advertising Models

Advertising revenue is a fundamental source of income for news portals. By exploring various advertising models, you can diversify your revenue streams and create a sustainable financial foundation. In this section, we will explore different advertising models and their nuances:

1. Display Advertising

Display advertising is one of the most common forms of online advertising:

- **Banner Ads**: Banner ads are graphical advertisements displayed prominently on your news portal. They come in various sizes and formats, including static images, animated GIFs, and rich media.

- **Ad Networks**: Partnering with ad networks like Google AdSense or Media.net allows you to display contextually relevant ads on your site. You earn revenue based on impressions (CPM) or clicks (CPC).

- **Direct Sales**: Selling ad space directly to advertisers or businesses can yield higher revenue, especially if you have a niche audience.

2. Native Advertising

Native advertising seamlessly integrates sponsored content with your news articles:

- **Sponsored Articles**: Create articles that resemble your regular content but are sponsored by advertisers. Ensure transparency by clearly labeling them as "sponsored."

- **Promoted Listings**: Incorporate promoted listings within article feeds, e-commerce sections, or directory-style pages.

- **In-Feed Ads**: Display ads that match the look and feel of your news feed, making them less intrusive and more engaging.

3. Video Advertising

Video advertising has gained prominence with the rise of video content consumption:

- **Pre-roll Ads**: These short video ads play before the main video content and offer a monetization opportunity for video-based news portals.

- **Mid-roll and Post-roll Ads**: Ads can also be inserted during or after video content, providing opportunities for additional revenue.

- **Sponsored Videos**: Collaborate with advertisers to create sponsored video content that aligns with your editorial focus.

4. Affiliate Marketing

Affiliate marketing involves promoting products or services and earning a commission on sales:

- **Product Reviews**: Write product reviews and include affiliate links to relevant products or services. Earn commissions on sales generated through your links.

- **Promotional Content**: Create content that promotes affiliate products or services, such as "best of" lists or buying guides.

5. Sponsored Content and Partnerships

Collaborate with brands and businesses for sponsored content:

- **Branded Content**: Work with advertisers to develop content that educates or entertains your audience while subtly promoting their products or services.

- **Partnerships**: Form long-term partnerships with brands for exclusive content creation or co-branded initiatives.

6. Subscription Models

While not strictly an advertising model, subscription-based revenue can complement your ad income:

- **Paywalls**: Implement paywalls that restrict access to premium content. Offer free content while requiring a subscription for full access.

- **Membership Programs**: Create membership programs that provide additional benefits to subscribers, such as ad-free browsing, exclusive content, or community access.

7. Email Marketing

Leverage your email subscriber list for advertising:

- **Sponsored Newsletters**: Include sponsored content or advertisements in your email newsletters sent to subscribers.

- **Affiliate Promotions**: Promote affiliate products or services via email campaigns, earning commissions on sales.

8. Mobile Advertising

With the increasing use of mobile devices, mobile advertising is essential:

- **In-App Ads**: If you have a mobile app, consider in-app advertising as an additional revenue source.

- **Mobile-Optimized Ads**: Ensure that your display and native ads are optimized for mobile devices to maximize user engagement.

Diversifying your advertising revenue streams allows you to mitigate risks associated with dependence on a single model. It's essential to balance revenue generation with user experience and ethical considerations. Transparency in labeling sponsored content and respecting user privacy are paramount to maintaining trust with your audience.

By carefully selecting and implementing the appropriate advertising models for your news portal, you can create a sustainable revenue strategy that supports your journalistic endeavors.

Section 9.2: Monetizing Your News Portal

Beyond Traditional Advertising

Exploring Alternative Revenue Streams

While traditional advertising models are a staple for news portals, diversifying your revenue sources can make your news portal more financially resilient. In this section, we will explore alternative strategies to monetize your news portal effectively:

1. Paid Subscriptions and Premium Content

- **Premium Articles**: Offer select articles, reports, or investigations as premium content accessible only to paid subscribers. These articles should provide unique and in-depth insights.

- **Tiered Subscriptions**: Create multiple subscription tiers, offering various levels of access. For instance, a basic tier might provide access to premium articles, while a premium tier could include exclusive content, ad-free browsing, and community access.

- **Membership Benefits**: Reward subscribers with additional benefits like early access to breaking news, member-only webinars, or discounts on merchandise.

2. E-books and Whitepapers

- **Publish E-books**: Compile your news portal's in-depth articles and investigations into e-books on relevant topics. These can be sold through platforms like Amazon Kindle or directly on your website.

- **Whitepapers**: Produce research-driven whitepapers related to your news coverage and sell them to businesses or professionals seeking industry insights.

3. Webinars and Online Courses

- **Host Webinars**: Organize webinars on current events or topics your audience is interested in. Charge a fee for access or provide them as a premium benefit to subscribers.

- **Online Courses**: Develop courses related to journalism, news writing, or media literacy. Sell these courses to individuals or educational institutions looking to enhance their skills.

4. Merchandise and Branded Products

- **News Portal Merchandise**: Create branded merchandise such as T-shirts, mugs, or tote bags featuring your news portal's logo or slogans. Sell these items through your website.

- **Bookstore**: Set up an online bookstore featuring books by your journalists or authors within your niche. You can earn commissions on book sales.

5. Crowdfunding and Donations

- **Crowdfunding Campaigns**: Launch crowdfunding campaigns on platforms like Kickstarter or Patreon. Offer exclusive perks to backers, such as personalized content or behind-the-scenes access.

- **Donation Requests**: Include donation requests on your website and in your content. Express the importance of supporting independent journalism and maintaining high editorial standards.

6. Sponsored Events and Workshops

- **Host Events**: Organize conferences, workshops, or panel discussions related to your news coverage. Attract sponsors and charge admission fees.

- **Sponsored Content**: Partner with businesses or organizations to host sponsored events or webinars on relevant topics. Generate revenue through sponsorships and ticket sales.

7. Consulting and Services

- **Journalism Workshops**: Offer workshops or consulting services to aspiring journalists or media organizations seeking guidance on improving their reporting practices.

- **Advisory Services**: Provide advisory services to businesses or policymakers on media and communication strategies based on your expertise.

8. Affiliate Marketing

- **Affiliate Programs**: Partner with affiliate programs related to your niche. Promote relevant products or services within your content, earning a commission on sales generated through your affiliate links.

9. Licensing and Syndication

- **Licensing Content**: License your content to other publications, websites, or media outlets, earning fees for content syndication.

- **Data and Research**: If you conduct extensive research or investigations, consider selling access to your data or research reports to businesses or researchers.

10. Community and Forum Access

- **Exclusive Forums**: Create exclusive forums or communities for your subscribers or dedicated readers. Charge a fee for access, providing a space for discussions and interactions.

11. Ad-Free Experience

- **Ad-Free Subscriptions**: Offer ad-free subscriptions to readers who prefer an uninterrupted reading experience. This can be an attractive option for those who find ads distracting.

Diversifying your revenue streams allows your news portal to adapt to changing market conditions and audience preferences. However, it's essential to maintain editorial independence and transparency while exploring these monetization strategies. Building a sustainable financial foundation for your news portal involves balancing the need for revenue with the commitment to high-quality journalism.

Section 9.3: Ad Placement and Optimization

Maximizing Revenue While Ensuring User Experience

Strategies for Effective Ad Placement and Optimization

Advertising plays a pivotal role in monetizing your news portal, but the way you implement it can greatly impact user experience and revenue generation. In this section, we will explore strategies for placing and optimizing ads on your news portal:

1. Understanding User Behavior

Before deciding on ad placements, it's essential to understand how users interact with your news portal:

- **Heatmaps and Analytics**: Use tools like heatmaps and web analytics to identify where users spend the most time on your site and where they tend to click.

- **User Surveys**: Conduct user surveys to gather feedback on ad placements and their impact on the reading experience.

2. Balanced Ad Density

While ads are essential for revenue, overcrowding your news portal with ads can deter readers:

- **Ad Density Testing**: Experiment with different ad densities to strike a balance between user experience and revenue. Avoid excessive ads that make your content hard to read.

- **Intrusive Ads**: Minimize intrusive ad formats like pop-ups or interstitials, which can lead to a poor user experience.

3. Native Advertising Integration

Integrating native ads seamlessly into your content can be effective:

- **In-Content Ads**: Place ads within the flow of your articles, making them appear like related content rather than traditional ads.

- **Ad Relevance**: Ensure that native ads align with the topic and tone of the surrounding content to enhance user engagement.

4. Above-the-Fold Placement

Content that's immediately visible when a user lands on your site is known as "above-the-fold." It's a prime location for ads:

- **Leaderboards**: Consider placing leaderboard ads at the top of your pages, but be cautious not to push valuable content too far down.

- **Top Sticky Ads**: Sticky ads that remain at the top of the screen as users scroll can also be effective.

5. Sidebar and Inline Ads

Sidebars and inline placements are commonly used for ads:

- **Sidebar Banners**: Utilize sidebar space for display ads that complement your content.

- **Inline Ads**: Insert inline ads within the text at strategic intervals, such as after the introduction or between sections.

6. Responsive Design

With users accessing news portals on various devices, responsive ad placement is crucial:

- **Mobile Optimization**: Ensure that ads are responsive and well-integrated into the mobile version of your news portal.

- **Ad Scaling**: Use scalable ad sizes that adjust to different screen dimensions.

7. A/B Testing

A/B testing allows you to compare different ad placements and formats:

- **Testing Elements**: Experiment with variations in ad size, placement, and format to determine which combinations yield the best results in terms of user engagement and revenue.

- **Performance Metrics**: Monitor key metrics like click-through rate (CTR) and revenue generated from each test to make data-driven decisions.

8. Ad Quality and Relevance

The quality and relevance of ads impact user engagement:

- **Ad Quality Checks**: Ensure that ads displayed on your site are of high quality and do not contain misleading or harmful content.

- **Targeted Advertising**: Implement targeted advertising to show users ads that are relevant to their interests, increasing the likelihood of clicks and conversions.

9. Ad Blocker Management

Some users may use ad blockers, which can affect your revenue:

- **Ad Blocker Detection**: Detect ad blockers and prompt users to disable them or subscribe to an ad-free experience.

- **Offer Ad-Free Subscriptions**: Provide users with the option to subscribe for an ad-free experience as an alternative to disabling ad blockers.

10. User Feedback and Transparency

User feedback is invaluable for optimizing ad placements:

- **Feedback Channels**: Establish channels for users to provide feedback on ad placements and report problematic ads.

- **Transparency**: Be transparent about your ad practices, clearly labeling sponsored content and disclosing your advertising policies.

Balancing ad placement for revenue generation and user experience is an ongoing process. Regularly review ad performance and seek feedback from your audience to refine your ad placement strategy. By prioritizing a positive user experience and delivering relevant, non-intrusive ads, you can maximize revenue while maintaining reader trust.

Chapter 10: Attracting Investors

Section 10.1: Preparing a Pitch

Crafting a Compelling Investment Pitch

Key Elements for a Successful Investor Pitch

Attracting investors is a critical step in securing the financial backing needed to grow and expand your news portal. In this section, we will explore the key elements and strategies for preparing a compelling investment pitch:

1. Understand Your Audience

- **Investor Profiling**: Begin by understanding the types of investors you are targeting. Are they venture capitalists, angel investors, or media industry experts? Tailor your pitch to their interests and priorities.

- **Investment Goals**: Consider what you need from investors beyond funding. Are you seeking strategic guidance, industry connections, or mentorship in addition to capital?

2. Craft a Compelling Story

- **Narrative Structure**: Your pitch should tell a compelling story that captures the essence of your news portal. Highlight your mission, vision, and the unique value your portal brings to the media landscape.

- **Problem-Solution Framework**: Address a specific problem or gap in the news industry and explain how your portal provides a solution.

3. Market Analysis and Opportunity

- **Market Research**: Provide a thorough analysis of the news market, including trends, competitors, and potential for growth. Investors want to see that you've done your homework.

- **Addressable Market**: Define your target audience and the size of the addressable market. Investors need to know the potential reach of your portal.

4. Revenue Model and Projections

- **Monetization Strategy**: Explain your revenue model, including advertising, subscriptions, or other income sources. Be clear about how you plan to generate revenue.

- **Financial Projections**: Present realistic financial projections, including revenue, expenses, and profitability forecasts. Investors want to see a clear path to return on their investment.

5. Team and Expertise

- **Team Introduction**: Introduce your core team members and their qualifications. Highlight any industry expertise, journalism awards, or relevant experience.

- **Roles and Responsibilities**: Clarify each team member's role and how their skills contribute to the success of the news portal.

6. Unique Value Proposition

- **Differentiation**: Explain what sets your news portal apart from competitors. Emphasize your unique value proposition, whether it's specialized reporting, a unique editorial voice, or a dedicated audience.

- **Barriers to Entry**: Address any barriers to entry that competitors might face, such as exclusive partnerships or proprietary technology.

7. Milestones and Roadmap

- **Milestone Achievements**: Showcase any significant milestones you've already achieved, such as audience growth, partnerships, or successful campaigns.

- **Roadmap**: Present a clear roadmap for the future, including expansion plans, content strategies, and technology enhancements.

8. Investment Ask

- **Funding Requirement**: Specify the amount of funding you are seeking and how you plan to utilize it. Break down the allocation of funds for different aspects of your news portal.

- **Equity Offer**: If you are offering equity in your company, be transparent about the percentage of ownership investors will receive in exchange for their investment.

9. Risk Assessment and Mitigation

- **Risk Awareness**: Acknowledge potential risks or challenges your news portal may face, whether they are related to industry changes, competition, or technology.

- **Mitigation Strategies**: Offer strategies for mitigating these risks and explain how investors can help address them.

10. Q&A Preparation

- **Anticipate Questions**: Prepare for potential questions investors may ask, both during and after your pitch. Be ready to provide detailed answers.

- **Backup Information**: Have supporting data, research, and documentation ready to substantiate your claims and projections.

11. Practice and Refine

- **Pitch Rehearsal**: Practice your pitch multiple times to ensure you can deliver it confidently and within the allotted time.

- **Feedback Loop**: Seek feedback from mentors, advisors, or peers to refine your pitch and address any weaknesses.

Remember that an investor pitch is not just about seeking funding; it's an opportunity to build relationships with individuals who believe in your vision. Tailor your pitch to align with your news portal's unique strengths and the specific interests of potential investors. Be passionate, confident, and authentic in presenting your case, and emphasize the potential for both financial returns and positive impact on the media industry.

Section 10.2: Identifying Potential Investors

Building a Network of Support

Strategies for Finding the Right Investors

Identifying and connecting with potential investors is a crucial step in securing funding for your news portal. In this section, we will explore strategies and methods for identifying and approaching the right investors:

1. Define Your Ideal Investor Profile

- **Investor Type**: Determine the type of investor that aligns with your news portal's needs. Are you seeking angel investors, venture capitalists, media industry experts, or strategic partners?

- **Investment Focus**: Consider whether your ideal investor has a specific focus, such as digital media, journalism, or technology. Look for investors whose interests align with your niche.

2. Tap into Your Existing Network

- **Personal Contacts**: Begin by reaching out to your personal and professional network. Friends, colleagues, mentors, or alumni connections may have valuable leads or introductions.

- **Industry Associations**: Join industry associations or journalism networks. Attend conferences, seminars, and events to network with potential investors who share your interests.

3. Online Platforms and Directories

- **Investor Databases**: Utilize online platforms and directories that connect entrepreneurs with investors. Websites like AngelList, Crunchbase, and Gust provide databases of potential investors.

- **Social Media**: Leverage professional social media platforms like LinkedIn to identify and connect with investors who have expressed interest in media and journalism.

4. Attend Pitch Events and Competitions

- **Startup Pitch Competitions**: Participate in startup pitch competitions and incubator programs. These events often attract investors looking for promising ventures.

- **Demo Days**: Attend accelerator or incubator demo days, where startups showcase their innovations to potential investors.

5. Engage with Investor Communities

- **Online Forums**: Join online forums and communities dedicated to startup funding and entrepreneurship. These platforms can help you identify potential investors and seek advice.

- **Angel Investor Groups**: Research local or regional angel investor groups that focus on media and journalism startups. These groups often have regular pitch sessions.

6. Seek Guidance from Mentors and Advisors

- **Mentor Networks**: Connect with mentors and advisors who have experience in fundraising. They can provide guidance on investor identification and pitch preparation.

- **Pitch Deck Review**: Ask experienced individuals to review your pitch deck and provide feedback to make it more appealing to investors.

7. Attend Industry Conferences

- **Media and Journalism Conferences**: Attend conferences specific to the media and journalism industry. These events attract professionals who may have an interest in supporting your news portal.

- **Networking Opportunities**: Make use of networking opportunities at these conferences to introduce your project to potential investors.

8. Research Investor Portfolios

- **Portfolio Analysis**: Study the portfolios of potential investors. Assess whether they have previously invested in media or journalism-related startups.

- **Investment History**: Research their investment history, including the stage at which they typically invest and the scale of their investments.

9. Personalized Outreach

- **Craft Personalized Messages**: When reaching out to potential investors, craft personalized messages that highlight why your news portal aligns with their interests and expertise.

- **Warm Introductions**: Whenever possible, seek warm introductions through mutual contacts. Warm introductions are more likely to yield positive responses.

10. Attend Investor Meetings and Seminars

- **Investor Meetings**: Attend investor meetings or seminars where you can learn more about the investment landscape and interact directly with potential investors.

- **Pitch Workshops**: Participate in pitch workshops or seminars to improve your pitch presentation skills and gain visibility among investors.

Identifying potential investors is a proactive process that involves research, networking, and personalized outreach. Building relationships with investors is often as important as securing their financial support, as they can provide valuable guidance and connections. Remember that investor identification is an ongoing effort, and persistence can lead to meaningful partnerships that benefit both your news portal and your investors.

Section 10.3: Pitching Your News Portal

Captivating Investors with Your Vision

Crafting an Impactful Pitch Presentation

Pitching your news portal is a critical step in attracting investors and securing the funding needed to bring your vision to life. In this section, we will explore the key elements and strategies for delivering a compelling pitch:

1. Structuring Your Pitch

- **Introduction**: Start with a concise and attention-grabbing introduction that highlights the core mission and value of your news portal. Set the stage for what investors can expect.

- **Problem Statement**: Clearly articulate the problem or gap in the news industry that your portal addresses. Use compelling statistics or real-life examples to illustrate the issue.

- **Solution**: Present your news portal as the solution to the problem you've identified. Explain how your platform fills the gap and meets the needs of your target audience.

2. Market Analysis and Opportunity

- **Market Insights**: Provide an in-depth analysis of the news market, including market trends, competitive landscape, and potential for growth.

Investors want to see that you've thoroughly researched your industry.

- **Target Audience**: Define your target audience and their demographics. Explain why your portal resonates with this audience and how you plan to capture their attention.

3. Monetization Strategy

- **Revenue Streams**: Clearly outline your monetization strategy, including advertising models, subscription plans, or other income sources. Investors need to understand how your portal generates revenue.

- **Financial Projections**: Present realistic financial projections, including revenue, expenses, and profitability forecasts. Investors want to see a clear path to a return on their investment.

4. Team and Expertise

- **Team Introduction**: Introduce the core members of your team and their qualifications. Highlight any industry expertise, awards, or relevant experience that makes your team well-suited to run the news portal.

- **Roles and Responsibilities**: Clearly define each team member's role and explain how their skills contribute to the success of the news portal.

5. Unique Value Proposition

- **Competitive Advantage**: Articulate what sets your news portal apart from competitors.

Emphasize your unique value proposition, whether it's specialized reporting, a unique editorial voice, or a dedicated audience.

- **Barriers to Entry**: Address any barriers to entry that competitors may face, such as exclusive partnerships or proprietary technology.

6. Milestones and Roadmap

- **Milestone Achievements**: Showcase any significant milestones your news portal has already achieved, such as audience growth, key partnerships, or successful campaigns.

- **Future Plans**: Present a clear roadmap for the future, including expansion plans, content strategies, and technology enhancements. Investors want to see that you have a vision for growth.

7. Investment Ask

- **Funding Requirement**: Specify the amount of funding you are seeking and how you plan to utilize it. Break down the allocation of funds for different aspects of your news portal.

- **Equity Offer**: If you are offering equity, be transparent about the percentage of ownership investors will receive in exchange for their investment.

8. Demonstrating Traction

- **User Engagement**: Highlight user engagement metrics, such as website traffic, user retention rates, or social media following. Demonstrating traction can build investor confidence.

- **Case Studies**: Share success stories or case studies related to your news portal's impact or partnerships that have contributed to its growth.

9. Addressing Investor Questions

- **Q&A Session**: Be prepared for a question and answer session following your pitch. Anticipate potential questions and have well-thought-out answers ready.

- **Backup Information**: Have supporting data, research, and documentation ready to substantiate your claims and projections.

10. Practice and Feedback

- **Pitch Rehearsal**: Practice your pitch multiple times to ensure a smooth and confident delivery. Time your presentation to fit within the allotted duration.

- **Feedback Loop**: Seek feedback from mentors, advisors, or peers who can provide valuable insights and help you refine your pitch.

11. Confidence and Passion

- **Confident Delivery**: Deliver your pitch with confidence and passion. Show that you believe in your news portal's potential and the positive impact it can have on the media industry.

- **Authenticity**: Be authentic and genuine in your presentation. Investors are not only evaluating your project but also the person behind it.

Remember that your pitch is not just about seeking funding; it's an opportunity to convey your passion, vision, and determination to potential investors who share your goals. Tailor your pitch to resonate with your audience, and be ready to adapt based on their feedback and questions. A well-crafted pitch can be the key to attracting the right investors who believe in your news portal's mission.

Chapter 11: Minimal Investment to Start

Section 11.1: Budgeting and Cost Analysis

Launching Your News Portal on a Shoestring Budget

Strategies for Efficient Budgeting

Starting a news portal on a limited budget requires careful planning and resource allocation. In this section, we will explore strategies for budgeting and analyzing costs to ensure a cost-effective launch:

1. Establish a Comprehensive Budget

- **Cost Categories**: Create a detailed budget that outlines all potential expenses. Common categories include web development, content creation, marketing, and operational costs.

- **Initial vs. Ongoing**: Distinguish between initial startup costs and ongoing operational expenses. This helps you allocate resources effectively.

2. Prioritize Essential Expenses

- **Minimum Viable Product (MVP)**: Identify the core features and components necessary for your news portal's MVP. Focus your budget on these essentials to get your portal up and running.

- **Cost-Effective Solutions**: Seek cost-effective solutions for web hosting, content management systems, and tools needed to minimize initial expenses.

3. Content Strategy and Production

- **In-House vs. Outsourcing**: Consider whether you can create content in-house or if outsourcing to freelance writers or contributors is more cost-effective.

- **Content Calendar**: Develop a content calendar to plan articles and stories in advance, optimizing the use of resources.

4. Website Development and Design

- **Ready-Made Themes**: Explore affordable ready-made website themes or templates for your content management system (CMS) to save on web development costs.

- **DIY vs. Professional**: Assess whether you can handle website setup and customization on your own or if hiring a web developer is necessary.

5. Marketing and Promotion

- **Social Media**: Utilize free or low-cost social media marketing to promote your news portal initially. Engage with your target audience on platforms where they are active.

- **Email Marketing**: Build an email list early on and leverage email marketing to reach your audience directly.

6. Monetization Strategy

- **Early Revenue Generation**: Consider implementing monetization strategies, such as targeted advertising or affiliate marketing, to start generating revenue as soon as possible.

- **Gradual Expansion**: Plan for the gradual expansion of monetization efforts as your audience grows.

7. Scalability

- **Scalable Solutions**: Choose tools, hosting, and services that can easily scale as your news portal's traffic and revenue increase. Avoid investing in resources you won't fully utilize at the outset.

8. Cost Analysis and Tracking

- **Expense Monitoring**: Continuously monitor your expenses and compare them to your budget. Identify areas where you can cut costs or reallocate resources.

- **Tools**: Use budgeting and expense tracking tools to streamline financial management.

9. Seek Low-Cost Resources

- **Free Resources**: Explore free or open-source software, plugins, and resources to minimize expenses.

- **Barter and Collaboration**: Consider bartering services or collaborating with other media professionals to share resources and reduce costs.

10. Adjust as You Grow

- **Flexibility**: Be prepared to adjust your budget and spending priorities as your news portal evolves. As revenue increases, consider reinvesting in content quality and audience engagement.

11. Financial Sustainability

- **Long-Term Viability**: Keep the long-term financial sustainability of your news portal in mind. Strive for a balance between minimizing costs and delivering quality journalism.

Launching a news portal on a minimal budget requires resourcefulness and a focus on essential elements. By carefully budgeting, prioritizing costs, and seeking cost-effective solutions, you can create a solid foundation for your news portal's growth. As your audience and revenue expand, you can gradually invest in additional features and resources to enhance the quality and reach of your portal.

Section 11.2: Cost-Effective Tools and Resources

Optimizing Your News Portal's Operations

Essential Tools for Cost-Efficient Operation

Running a news portal on a tight budget requires leveraging cost-effective tools and resources. In this section, we will explore essential tools and strategies to optimize your portal's operations:

1. Content Management Systems (CMS)

- **WordPress**: Consider using WordPress as your CMS, which offers a free and user-friendly platform for publishing content. There are numerous free and premium themes available to customize your website's look.

- **Open-Source CMS**: Explore open-source CMS options like Joomla or Drupal, which provide flexibility and cost savings compared to proprietary systems.

2. Website Hosting

- **Shared Hosting**: In the initial stages, shared hosting plans are cost-effective options. They allow multiple websites to share server resources, reducing hosting expenses.

- **Cloud Hosting**: Consider cloud hosting providers like AWS, Google Cloud, or DigitalOcean, where you can scale resources as your portal grows, minimizing upfront costs.

3. Content Creation

- **Open-Source Graphics Tools**: Use open-source graphics software like GIMP or Inkscape for image editing and graphic design, eliminating the need for expensive graphic design software.

- **Freelance Writers**: Hire freelance writers or contributors on a per-article basis rather than maintaining a full-time writing team.

4. Social Media Management

- **Free Social Media Tools**: Utilize free social media management tools like Hootsuite or Buffer to schedule posts and track engagement across multiple platforms.

- **Engagement Analytics**: Monitor social media analytics to identify which platforms are most effective in reaching your audience, allowing you to focus your efforts.

5. Email Marketing

- **Email Marketing Platforms**: Use cost-effective email marketing platforms like Mailchimp or SendinBlue for building and managing your email subscriber list.

- **Automation**: Implement email automation to send targeted messages to your audience based on their interests and behavior.

6. Analytics and SEO

- **Google Analytics**: Utilize Google Analytics for in-depth website traffic analysis and user behavior insights. It's a free tool that provides valuable data.

- **SEO Tools**: Use free or low-cost SEO tools like Moz, SEMrush, or Ubersuggest to optimize your content for search engines.

7. Collaborative Tools

- **Cloud-Based Collaboration**: Leverage cloud-based collaboration tools like Google Workspace (formerly G Suite) for document sharing and real-time collaboration among your team.

- **Project Management**: Use free project management tools like Trello or Asana to organize tasks, assignments, and project timelines.

8. Monetization Solutions

- **Ad Networks**: Partner with cost-effective advertising networks like Google AdSense or Media.net to monetize your content through display ads.

- **Affiliate Marketing**: Explore affiliate marketing programs related to your niche to earn commissions on product or service referrals.

9. Learning and Training

- **Online Courses**: Instead of formal training, consider online courses and tutorials available on platforms like Coursera, Udemy, or LinkedIn Learning to acquire new skills.

- **Industry Webinars**: Attend industry webinars and virtual events, which often offer valuable insights at a fraction of the cost of physical conferences.

10. Legal and Compliance

- **Legal Templates**: Utilize free or low-cost legal document templates for privacy policies, terms of service, and disclaimers to ensure legal compliance.

- **Self-Education**: Stay informed about legal and compliance requirements relevant to your news portal to avoid costly legal issues.

11. Data Backup and Security

- **Automated Backups**: Implement automated backup solutions to protect your content and data without the need for expensive IT services.

- **Security Plugins**: Use cost-effective security plugins and tools to enhance website security and protect against cyber threats.

By incorporating these cost-effective tools and resources into your news portal's operations, you can maintain efficiency and quality while keeping expenses in check. It's important to regularly review and assess your toolkit to ensure that it aligns with your portal's evolving needs and budget constraints.

Section 11.3: Scaling Up Gradually

Sustaining Growth on a Limited Budget

Strategies for Sustainable Growth

Gradually scaling up your news portal allows you to grow sustainably without straining your limited budget. In this section, we will explore strategies and considerations for gradual expansion:

1. Content Quality and Quantity

- **Focus on Core Topics**: Concentrate your efforts on covering core topics within your niche. Producing high-quality content on these subjects establishes your portal's expertise.

- **Regular Posting**: Maintain a consistent posting schedule, even if it means publishing fewer articles initially. Quality should take precedence over quantity.

2. Audience Engagement

- **Community Building**: Foster a sense of community among your readers. Encourage comments, discussions, and interactions to build a loyal audience.

- **User-Generated Content**: Consider involving your audience in content creation through user-generated content, such as guest posts or reader contributions.

3. Monetization Strategies

- **Diversify Revenue Streams**: As your portal grows, explore additional monetization options beyond advertising, such as sponsored content, premium memberships, or events.

- **Optimize Existing Revenue Sources**: Continuously analyze the performance of your existing revenue streams and fine-tune them for better results.

4. SEO and Organic Growth

- **Keyword Research**: Conduct ongoing keyword research to identify new opportunities for ranking in search engine results pages (SERPs).

- **Content Optimization**: Optimize existing content for search engines to maximize organic traffic without significant additional costs.

5. Partnerships and Collaborations

- **Content Syndication**: Partner with other media outlets or websites for content syndication, allowing you to reach wider audiences without creating entirely new content.

- **Cross-Promotions**: Collaborate with complementary businesses or websites for mutually beneficial promotions and cross-links.

6. Analytics and Data-Driven Decisions

- **Performance Tracking**: Continuously monitor website analytics to identify trends, popular content, and areas for improvement. Use data to inform your growth strategy.

- **A/B Testing**: Experiment with A/B testing to refine website elements, such as headlines, call-to-action buttons, or ad placements, to improve user engagement and conversions.

7. Audience Feedback

- **Feedback Loops**: Encourage feedback from your audience through surveys, comments, or social media interactions. Use this feedback to make informed improvements.

- **Iterative Changes**: Implement changes based on audience feedback incrementally, rather than costly overhauls.

8. Outsourcing and Delegation

- **Outsourcing Tasks**: Consider outsourcing specific tasks or roles, such as content creation, social media management, or SEO, to freelancers or agencies as revenue allows.

- **Virtual Assistants**: Virtual assistants can handle administrative tasks, freeing up your time to focus on strategic growth initiatives.

9. Reinvestment of Profits

- **Smart Reinvestment**: When revenue allows, reinvest a portion of your profits back into the portal. This can fund additional content, marketing efforts, or technology upgrades.

- **Prioritized Investments**: Prioritize investments that directly contribute to revenue generation and audience growth.

10. Collaborative Growth

- **Collaborative Ventures**: Explore collaborative ventures with other media entities or startups that share similar goals. Joint projects can expand your reach and resources.

- **Shared Resources**: Consider shared resources, such as marketing tools or software licenses, with collaborative partners to reduce individual costs.

11. Scalable Infrastructure

- **Infrastructure Planning**: As you grow, invest in infrastructure that can easily scale with your portal's increasing demands, ensuring minimal downtime or disruption.

- **Cloud Solutions**: Cloud-based services can be scaled up or down as needed, offering flexibility and cost-efficiency.

Gradual growth is a prudent approach for a news portal operating on a limited budget. It allows you to refine your strategies, learn from your audience, and make informed decisions while maintaining financial stability. As your news portal gains traction and generates more revenue, you can strategically reinvest in its expansion and further strengthen its position in the industry.

Section 11.3: Scaling Up Gradually

Sustaining Growth on a Limited Budget

Strategies for Sustainable Growth

Gradually scaling up your news portal allows you to grow sustainably without straining your limited budget. In this section, we will explore strategies and considerations for gradual expansion:

1. Content Quality and Quantity

- **Focus on Core Topics**: Concentrate your efforts on covering core topics within your niche. Producing high-quality content on these subjects establishes your portal's expertise.

- **Regular Posting**: Maintain a consistent posting schedule, even if it means publishing fewer articles initially. Quality should take precedence over quantity.

2. Audience Engagement

- **Community Building**: Foster a sense of community among your readers. Encourage comments, discussions, and interactions to build a loyal audience.

- **User-Generated Content**: Consider involving your audience in content creation through user-generated content, such as guest posts or reader contributions.

3. Monetization Strategies

- **Diversify Revenue Streams**: As your portal grows, explore additional monetization options beyond advertising, such as sponsored content, premium memberships, or events.

- **Optimize Existing Revenue Sources**: Continuously analyze the performance of your existing revenue streams and fine-tune them for better results.

4. SEO and Organic Growth

- **Keyword Research**: Conduct ongoing keyword research to identify new opportunities for ranking in search engine results pages (SERPs).

- **Content Optimization**: Optimize existing content for search engines to maximize organic traffic without significant additional costs.

5. Partnerships and Collaborations

- **Content Syndication**: Partner with other media outlets or websites for content syndication, allowing you to reach wider audiences without creating entirely new content.

- **Cross-Promotions**: Collaborate with complementary businesses or websites for mutually beneficial promotions and cross-links.

6. Analytics and Data-Driven Decisions

- **Performance Tracking**: Continuously monitor website analytics to identify trends, popular content, and areas for improvement. Use data to inform your growth strategy.

- **A/B Testing**: Experiment with A/B testing to refine website elements, such as headlines, call-to-action buttons, or ad placements, to improve user engagement and conversions.

7. Audience Feedback

- **Feedback Loops**: Encourage feedback from your audience through surveys, comments, or social media interactions. Use this feedback to make informed improvements.

- **Iterative Changes**: Implement changes based on audience feedback incrementally, rather than costly overhauls.

8. Outsourcing and Delegation

- **Outsourcing Tasks**: Consider outsourcing specific tasks or roles, such as content creation, social media management, or SEO, to freelancers or agencies as revenue allows.

- **Virtual Assistants**: Virtual assistants can handle administrative tasks, freeing up your time to focus on strategic growth initiatives.

9. Reinvestment of Profits

- **Smart Reinvestment**: When revenue allows, reinvest a portion of your profits back into the portal. This can fund additional content, marketing efforts, or technology upgrades.

- **Prioritized Investments**: Prioritize investments that directly contribute to revenue generation and audience growth.

10. Collaborative Growth

- **Collaborative Ventures**: Explore collaborative ventures with other media entities or startups that share similar goals. Joint projects can expand your reach and resources.

- **Shared Resources**: Consider shared resources, such as marketing tools or software licenses, with collaborative partners to reduce individual costs.

11. Scalable Infrastructure

- **Infrastructure Planning**: As you grow, invest in infrastructure that can easily scale with your portal's increasing demands, ensuring minimal downtime or disruption.

- **Cloud Solutions**: Cloud-based services can be scaled up or down as needed, offering flexibility and cost-efficiency.

Gradual growth is a prudent approach for a news portal operating on a limited budget. It allows you to refine your strategies, learn from your audience, and make informed decisions while maintaining financial stability. As your news portal gains traction and generates more revenue, you can strategically reinvest in its expansion and further strengthen its position in the industry.

Chapter 12: Special Assignment Stories

Section 12.1: Investigative Journalism

Uncovering Truth and Holding Power Accountable

Mastering the Art of Investigative Reporting

Investigative journalism is a pillar of quality news reporting, where in-depth research and analysis uncover hidden truths and expose wrongdoing. In this section, we will delve into the essential aspects of investigative journalism:

1. Defining Investigative Journalism

- **In-Depth Reporting**: Investigative journalism involves thorough research, fact-checking, and analysis to uncover information not readily accessible to the public.

- **Public Interest**: It focuses on stories of public interest, often exposing corruption, abuse of power, or issues that significantly impact society.

2. Research and Source Building

- **Primary Sources**: Investigative journalists often rely on primary sources, such as confidential informants, documents, and whistleblowers, to access exclusive information.

- **Source Protection**: Understand the importance of source protection and legal considerations when dealing with sensitive information.

3. Story Selection

- **Impactful Issues**: Choose investigative topics that have a significant societal impact, addressing issues that resonate with your audience.

- **Story Feasibility**: Assess the feasibility of the investigation, considering resource allocation and potential outcomes.

4. Research and Data Analysis

- **Document Verification**: Thoroughly verify documents and evidence to ensure accuracy and authenticity.

- **Data Mining**: Utilize data mining techniques to extract valuable insights from large datasets, especially in data-driven investigations.

5. Ethical Considerations

- **Accuracy and Fairness**: Maintain the highest standards of accuracy and fairness in investigative reporting to uphold the credibility of your news portal.

- **Legal and Privacy**: Adhere to legal and ethical guidelines, respecting privacy and consent while pursuing sensitive stories.

6. Writing and Storytelling

- **Narrative Craftsmanship**: Craft compelling narratives that engage readers and provide a clear understanding of the investigation's findings.

- **Transparency**: Clearly present your methodology and sources to build trust with your audience.

7. Safety and Security

- **Journalist Safety**: Ensure the safety of investigative journalists, especially in cases that may involve threats or intimidation.

- **Digital Security**: Implement digital security measures to protect sensitive information and sources.

8. Legal Protections

- **Shield Laws**: Understand the shield laws and legal protections available to journalists, which vary by jurisdiction.

- **Libel and Defamation**: Be vigilant in avoiding libel and defamation claims by maintaining factual reporting.

9. Collaborations and Partnerships

- **Collaborative Investigations**: Collaborate with other news organizations or journalists on complex investigations to leverage resources and expertise.

- **Media Partnerships**: Establish partnerships with media outlets for broader reach and impact.

10. Impact Assessment

- **Measuring Impact**: Assess the impact of your investigative reporting through tangible outcomes, such as policy changes, legal actions, or public awareness.

- **Continuous Follow-Up**: Continue to follow up on investigative stories, tracking developments and holding accountable those responsible for wrongdoing.

11. Challenges and Risks

- **Legal Threats**: Be prepared for potential legal threats and lawsuits from subjects of investigative reporting.

- **Resource Intensiveness**: Investigative journalism can be resource-intensive; plan accordingly to allocate resources effectively.

12. Building Credibility

- **Credibility**: Building and maintaining credibility is crucial for investigative journalists. Transparent sourcing and fact-checking enhance your portal's reputation.

- **Editorial Oversight**: Establish editorial oversight and ethical guidelines specific to investigative journalism within your news portal.

13. Impactful Stories

- **Impactful Reporting**: Share impactful investigative stories with your audience, emphasizing their significance and societal relevance.

- **Reader Engagement**: Encourage reader engagement and feedback on investigative stories, fostering a sense of community involvement.

Investigative journalism is a powerful tool for news portals, contributing to the public's right to know and holding those in power accountable. While it presents challenges, the pursuit of truth and the commitment to ethical reporting are at the core of this essential aspect of journalism.

Section 12.2: Feature Stories and Interviews

Captivating Your Audience with In-Depth Content

Mastering Feature Storytelling and Interviewing

Feature stories and interviews offer an opportunity to connect with your audience on a personal level, providing in-depth insights and engaging narratives. In this section, we will delve into the essential aspects of feature stories and interviews:

1. Feature Stories: Crafting Engaging Narratives

- **Narrative Structure**: Use storytelling techniques to structure feature stories, with a clear beginning, middle, and end. Engage readers emotionally.

- **Character Development**: Highlight compelling characters or subjects within your feature stories to create a human connection.

2. Story Selection

- **Human Interest**: Feature stories often focus on human experiences, unique personalities, or stories that resonate emotionally with your audience.

- **Relevance**: Choose feature story topics that align with your news portal's niche and the interests of your readers.

3. Research and Preparation

- **Thorough Research**: Conduct thorough research on the subject of your feature story or interview to gather background information and context.

- **Interview Preparation**: Prepare insightful questions and a structured interview format to ensure a productive and engaging conversation.

4. Conducting Interviews

- **Active Listening**: Practice active listening during interviews, allowing your subjects to express themselves fully while guiding the conversation.

- **Follow-Up Questions**: Ask follow-up questions to dig deeper into the subject's experiences or insights.

5. Ethical Considerations

- **Privacy and Consent**: Respect the privacy and obtain consent from interviewees, especially when discussing personal or sensitive matters.

- **Transparency**: Clearly disclose any potential conflicts of interest or affiliations that may impact the objectivity of your feature story or interview.

6. Writing and Presentation

- **Engaging Writing**: Craft feature stories with engaging writing that draws readers into the narrative.

- **Interview Transcripts**: If publishing interviews in written form, provide accurate and well-formatted transcripts for clarity.

7. Multimedia Elements

- **Visuals**: Enhance feature stories with relevant visuals, such as photographs, videos, or infographics.

- **Audio and Video Interviews**: Consider recording and sharing audio or video interviews to provide a more immersive experience for your audience.

8. Impact and Human Connection

- **Emotion and Empathy**: Feature stories and interviews should evoke emotion and empathy, allowing readers to connect with the subject on a personal level.

- **Inspiration**: Highlight positive stories or inspirational journeys to uplift and motivate your audience.

9. Diversity and Inclusivity

- **Diverse Perspectives**: Seek out a diverse range of interviewees and feature story subjects to reflect a variety of voices and experiences.

- **Inclusivity**: Ensure that your feature stories and interviews are inclusive and respectful of all backgrounds and perspectives.

10. Engaging the Audience

- **Interactive Elements**: Encourage reader engagement by incorporating interactive elements such as polls, quizzes, or discussion forums related to your feature content.

- **Feedback and Comments**: Encourage readers to share their thoughts and feedback on feature stories and interviews, fostering community interaction.

11. Measuring Impact

- **Audience Engagement Metrics**: Analyze audience engagement metrics, such as comments, shares, and time spent on feature content, to gauge its impact.

- **Feedback Loop**: Use reader feedback to improve your feature storytelling and interview techniques continually.

Feature stories and interviews provide an opportunity to dive deep into compelling narratives and connect with your audience on a personal level. When executed effectively, they can captivate readers, inspire empathy, and contribute to your news portal's overall quality and appeal.

Section 12.3: Balancing Breaking News and In-Depth Reporting

Navigating the Fast-Paced World of Journalism

Strategies for Effective Coverage

Balancing breaking news and in-depth reporting is a critical aspect of news portal management. In this section, we will delve into strategies for finding equilibrium:

1. The Role of Breaking News

- **Timeliness**: Breaking news stories are time-sensitive and require immediate reporting to keep your audience informed in real-time.

- **Alerts and Notifications**: Implement alert systems or push notifications to promptly notify your audience of breaking developments.

2. In-Depth Reporting: The Value of Context

- **Contextualization**: In-depth reporting provides context and analysis, helping readers understand the broader implications of news events.

- **Background Information**: Include background information in in-depth reports to give readers a comprehensive understanding of complex topics.

3. Prioritizing News Coverage

- **Editorial Judgment**: Develop a clear editorial judgment process to determine when a story warrants immediate breaking news coverage and when it's suitable for in-depth reporting.

- **Hierarchy of Importance**: Create a hierarchy of news importance within your newsroom to allocate resources efficiently.

4. Resource Allocation

- **Dedicated Teams**: Assign dedicated teams or reporters to handle breaking news and separate teams for in-depth reporting.

- **Flexible Staffing**: Consider flexible staffing arrangements to allocate resources as needed during peak news cycles.

5. Collaboration and Cross-Training

- **Cross-Training**: Train reporters to excel in both breaking news and in-depth reporting, ensuring flexibility within your newsroom.

- **Collaboration**: Encourage collaboration between teams to share insights and findings, enriching both types of reporting.

6. Real-Time Updates

- **Updating In-Depth Stories**: For major breaking news events, update related in-depth stories in real-time to provide readers with the latest context and analysis.

- **Transparency**: Clearly communicate updates to readers to maintain transparency and credibility.

7. Diverse Content Formats

- **Breaking News Formats**: Utilize concise and straightforward formats for breaking news, such as short articles or bullet-point summaries.

- **In-Depth Formats**: In-depth reports can be presented in longer articles, multimedia features, or series that allow for comprehensive exploration.

8. Audience Engagement

- **Audience Feedback**: Encourage audience feedback to understand their preferences for news coverage and use it to refine your strategy.

- **Interactive Elements**: Include interactive elements, such as polls or surveys, to gauge audience interest in various topics.

9. Editorial Calendar

- **Planning**: Maintain an editorial calendar that outlines the balance between breaking news coverage and planned in-depth reports.

- **Flexibility**: Be prepared to adapt the calendar based on unforeseen developments.

10. Measuring Impact

- **Audience Metrics**: Analyze audience metrics to evaluate the performance and impact of both breaking news and in-depth reporting.

- **Reader Behavior**: Monitor reader behavior, such as time spent on articles and shares, to understand content preferences.

Balancing breaking news and in-depth reporting is a dynamic process that requires agility and strategic planning. By aligning your news portal's goals with audience expectations and maintaining a flexible approach to coverage, you can effectively serve your readers in both fast-paced and deep-dive news environments.

Chapter 13: Using Images and Videos

Section 13.1: Sourcing and Licensing Visual Content

Ensuring Quality and Compliance

Effective Strategies for Visual Content Management

Visual content, including images and videos, plays a crucial role in engaging your audience and conveying information. In this section, we will delve into strategies for sourcing and licensing visual content:

1. Sourcing Visual Content

- **Original Content**: Encourage your in-house photographers and videographers to capture original visual content related to news events. This can enhance your portal's unique identity.

- **Stock Agencies**: Partner with reputable stock image and video agencies to access a vast library of professionally produced visuals.

- **User-Generated Content (UGC)**: Engage with your audience to submit user-generated visuals, provided they have proper permissions and rights.

2. Licensing and Copyright

- **Understanding Licensing**: Familiarize yourself with various types of licenses, including royalty-free, rights-managed, and creative commons, to determine how you can use visuals legally.

- **Public Domain**: Explore public domain resources where visuals are not under copyright protection and can be freely used for any purpose.

- **Fair Use**: Understand the concept of fair use, which allows limited use of copyrighted material for purposes like news reporting, provided it meets certain criteria.

3. Compliance and Permissions

- **Model Releases**: When using visuals containing identifiable individuals, ensure you have proper model releases or permissions for their use.

- **Property Releases**: For visuals featuring private property or trademarks, secure property releases when necessary to avoid legal issues.

4. Attribution and Crediting

- **Proper Attribution**: If a particular license requires attribution, ensure you provide accurate credit to the content creator or source.

- **Maintaining Credibility**: Proper attribution and crediting also contribute to your portal's credibility and transparency.

5. Image and Video Editing

- **Editing Guidelines**: Establish clear guidelines for editing visuals to maintain their integrity and accuracy, especially when cropping or altering images.

- **Authenticity**: Maintain authenticity by clearly labeling visuals that have been manipulated or enhanced.

6. Metadata and Organization

- **Metadata Management**: Implement a robust system for tagging, cataloging, and organizing visual content with metadata, making it easy to retrieve and track usage.

- **Rights Management**: Keep detailed records of licensing agreements and usage rights associated with each visual.

7. Content Verification

- **Fact-Check Visuals**: Ensure the accuracy of visuals, especially when they depict events or scenes related to news stories.

- **Reverse Image Search**: Use reverse image search tools to verify the authenticity and source of visuals.

8. Accessibility and Inclusivity

- **Alt Text**: Provide alt text for images and videos to make content accessible to individuals with disabilities.

- **Diverse Representation**: Seek visuals that represent diverse backgrounds, cultures, and perspectives to promote inclusivity.

9. Ethical Considerations

- **Sensitivity**: Exercise sensitivity when using visuals related to sensitive or tragic events, considering the potential impact on your audience.

- **Avoiding Exploitation**: Avoid sensationalizing or exploiting distressing visuals for the sake of clickbait.

10. Content Monetization

- **Monetization Strategies**: Explore ways to monetize visual content, such as offering premium visual packages to subscribers or licensing content to other outlets.

- **Balancing Revenue and Ethics**: Ensure that your monetization efforts align with ethical practices and respect for copyrights.

11. Training and Guidelines

- **Staff Training**: Train your staff, including editors and content creators, on visual content usage guidelines and legal considerations.

- **Regular Updates**: Keep your team updated on changes in copyright laws and best practices for visual content usage.

Effective management of visual content is essential for maintaining the quality, credibility, and legal compliance of your news portal. By following these strategies and staying informed about licensing and copyright issues, you can enhance the visual appeal of your portal while respecting the rights of content creators.

Section 13.2: Creating Engaging Multimedia Content

Enhancing News Delivery

Strategies for Multimedia Storytelling

Multimedia content offers a dynamic way to convey news stories and engage your audience. In this section, we will delve into strategies for creating engaging multimedia content:

1. Video Production

- **Storyboarding**: Develop clear storyboards or scripts before shooting to maintain a structured narrative and efficient use of resources.

- **Visual Storytelling**: Utilize visuals, interviews, and narration to craft compelling video stories that resonate with your audience.

2. Infographics and Data Visualization

- **Data Interpretation**: Use infographics to simplify complex data and statistics, making them accessible and engaging for readers.

- **Interactive Infographics**: Create interactive infographics that allow users to explore data and gain deeper insights.

3. Interactive Features

- **Interactive Maps**: Incorporate interactive maps to provide context for location-based stories or events.

- **Data Tools**: Build interactive data tools that enable readers to customize data queries and explore trends.

4. Animation and Motion Graphics

- **Explainer Videos**: Use animation and motion graphics for explainer videos that break down complex topics into digestible segments.

- **Visual Appeal**: Ensure that animation enhances the visual appeal of your content without overwhelming the message.

5. Podcasts and Audio Stories

- **Narrative Podcasts**: Create narrative podcasts that tell stories through audio, using compelling narration and sound design.

- **Interview Series**: Develop interview series to provide in-depth insights into various topics or personalities.

6. Live Streaming and Webinars

- **Live Reporting**: Utilize live streaming for real-time reporting of events, interviews, or breaking news.

- **Educational Webinars**: Host webinars to educate your audience on specific subjects related to news stories.

7. Accessibility and Inclusivity

- **Transcripts**: Provide transcripts for multimedia content to accommodate individuals with hearing impairments and enhance SEO.

- **Captioning**: Caption videos to make content accessible to a broader audience.

8. Quality and Production

- **Professional Equipment**: Invest in professional audio and video equipment to ensure high production quality.

- **Editing and Post-Production**: Allocate time for thorough editing and post-production to enhance the overall quality of your multimedia content.

9. Storytelling Excellence

- **Narrative Flow**: Maintain a cohesive narrative flow in multimedia content, guiding the audience through the story seamlessly.

- **Engaging Script**: Write engaging scripts and voiceovers that capture the essence of the story and hold the audience's attention.

10. Social Media Integration

- **Platform Compatibility**: Optimize multimedia content for various social media platforms to maximize reach and engagement.

- **Cross-Promotion**: Promote multimedia content across your news portal's social media channels to attract a broader audience.

11. Analytics and Feedback

- **Audience Engagement**: Monitor audience engagement metrics for multimedia content to understand what resonates with your readers.

- **Feedback Loop**: Encourage audience feedback and use it to refine your multimedia storytelling strategies continually.

12. Ethical Considerations

- **Sensitive Visuals**: Approach the use of sensitive visuals or multimedia content related to tragic events with empathy and caution.

- **Transparency**: Clearly disclose any potential biases or affiliations when presenting multimedia content related to news stories.

Effective multimedia storytelling can set your news portal apart by providing diverse and engaging ways for readers to consume information. By implementing these strategies, you can leverage the power of multimedia to enhance your news delivery and captivate your audience.

Section 13.3: Optimizing Media for Web
Enhancing Performance and User Experience
Best Practices for Web-Ready Media

Optimizing media for web usage is crucial to maintain a fast, user-friendly news portal. In this section, we will delve into best practices for optimizing images and videos:

1. Image Optimization

- **Resolution and Compression**: Resize images to the appropriate dimensions and compress them to reduce file size while maintaining quality. Use web-friendly image formats like JPEG and PNG.

- **Responsive Images**: Implement responsive design techniques to serve different image sizes based on the user's device, ensuring optimal viewing on desktop and mobile.

2. Video Optimization

- **Format Selection**: Choose video formats like MP4 or WebM that are widely supported by web browsers and provide good compression without compromising quality.

- **Resolution and Bitrate**: Adjust video resolution and bitrate settings to balance quality with fast loading times. Use adaptive streaming for variable internet connections.

3. Lazy Loading

- **Deferred Loading**: Employ lazy loading techniques to load images and videos only when they come into the user's viewport, reducing initial page load times.

- **Lazy Loading Plugins**: Consider using lazy loading plugins or libraries for effortless implementation.

4. Content Delivery Networks (CDNs)

- **CDN Integration**: Utilize CDNs to distribute media files across multiple servers, reducing latency and improving load times for users across the globe.

- **CDN Optimization**: Configure your CDN to automatically optimize images and videos on the fly, further enhancing performance.

5. Image and Video Tags

- **Alt Text**: Provide descriptive alt text for images to ensure accessibility and improve SEO.

- **Title and Description**: Include meaningful titles and descriptions for videos to enhance search engine visibility.

6. Caching Mechanisms

- **Browser Caching**: Leverage browser caching to store media files locally on users' devices, reducing the need for repeated downloads.

- **Content Caching**: Implement content caching at the server level to deliver media files quickly to returning visitors.

7. Image Sprites

- **Sprite Creation**: Combine small images, icons, or graphics into sprite sheets to minimize the number of HTTP requests.

- **CSS Sprites**: Use CSS techniques to display specific parts of the sprite sheet as needed.

8. Minification

- **Code Minification**: Minify HTML, CSS, and JavaScript code to reduce file sizes and improve page loading speed.

- **Plugin Usage**: Employ minification plugins or tools to automate the process.

9. Testing and Monitoring

- **Performance Testing**: Regularly test your news portal's performance using tools like Google PageSpeed Insights or GTmetrix to identify and address optimization opportunities.

- **Monitoring Tools**: Implement monitoring tools to track loading times and user experience, promptly addressing any issues.

10. Mobile Optimization

- **Responsive Design**: Ensure that images and videos adapt to various screen sizes, orientations, and resolutions to provide a seamless mobile experience.

- **Mobile-First Approach**: Prioritize mobile optimization during media selection and placement.

11. Ethical Considerations

- **Visual Integrity**: Maintain the visual integrity of images and videos during optimization, avoiding excessive compression that may degrade quality.

- **Content Accuracy**: Verify that media optimization doesn't alter the accuracy or context of news content.

Optimizing media for the web is essential for keeping your news portal responsive and user-friendly. By following these best practices and regularly monitoring your portal's performance, you can provide a seamless multimedia experience for your readers while maintaining fast loading times.

Chapter 14: Promoting Your News Portal

Section 14.1: Marketing Strategies

Building Awareness and Audience Engagement

Proven Marketing Tactics for News Portals

Marketing is a fundamental aspect of growing your news portal's audience and influence. In this section, we will delve into marketing strategies tailored to news portals:

1. Content Promotion

- **Content Syndication**: Collaborate with other news outlets or aggregators to syndicate your content, expanding its reach to a wider audience.

- **Email Marketing**: Build and nurture an email subscriber list to distribute newsletters containing top stories and exclusive content.

2. Social Media Engagement

- **Platform Selection**: Identify the social media platforms most frequented by your target audience and maintain an active presence there.

- **Engagement Strategies**: Develop engagement strategies, such as live streaming, polls, and interactive content, to foster a loyal social media community.

3. Search Engine Optimization (SEO)

- **Keyword Research**: Conduct thorough keyword research to identify the most relevant and high-traffic keywords related to your news niche.

- **On-Page SEO**: Optimize your articles and content for search engines by strategically incorporating keywords and metadata.

4. Paid Advertising

- **Pay-Per-Click (PPC)**: Invest in PPC advertising campaigns on platforms like Google Ads or social media to drive targeted traffic.

- **Remarketing**: Implement remarketing campaigns to re-engage users who have previously visited your portal.

5. Influencer Partnerships

- **Collaborations**: Partner with industry influencers or experts for guest contributions, interviews, or endorsements to boost credibility.

- **Affiliate Partnerships**: Explore affiliate marketing partnerships that align with your news niche to generate additional revenue.

6. Email Marketing

Segmentation: Segment your email list to send tailored content and recommendations based on subscriber interests and behaviors.

- **Automation**: Implement email automation for personalized onboarding sequences, newsletters, and content updates.

7. Analytics and Data-Driven Decisions

- **Monitoring Metrics**: Continuously monitor website analytics, social media insights, and email performance to make data-driven decisions.

- **A/B Testing**: Conduct A/B tests to optimize headlines, visuals, and calls to action for better engagement.

8. Community Building

- **Online Forums**: Create or participate in online forums and communities relevant to your news niche to establish your portal as an authoritative source.

- **Comment Engagement**: Engage with reader comments on your articles to foster discussion and build a sense of community.

9. Offline Promotion

- **Media Partnerships**: Forge partnerships with local or regional media outlets for cross-promotion through events, print publications, or broadcasts.

- **Networking**: Attend industry conferences and events to connect with influencers, potential partners, and readers.

10. Ethical Marketing

- **Transparency**: Maintain transparency in marketing practices, clearly distinguishing between editorial content and sponsored content.

- **Fact-Checking**: Ensure that marketing materials, including advertisements, adhere to ethical and factual standards.

11. Mobile Optimization

- **Mobile-First Design**: Ensure that your news portal is fully optimized for mobile devices, as an increasing number of users access news on smartphones and tablets.

- **Mobile Advertising**: Implement mobile-specific advertising strategies, such as location-based targeting, for mobile users.

12. Crisis Management

- **Preparedness**: Develop a crisis management plan to address potential issues, including misinformation or reputation crises.

- **Swift Responses**: Respond promptly to any crisis or negative publicity with transparency and corrective actions.

Effective marketing strategies are essential for increasing the visibility and impact of your news portal. By employing these tactics and staying attuned to your audience's preferences, you can foster growth and engage a wider readership.

Section 14.2: Building a Community

Fostering Engagement and Loyalty

Strategies for Community Building

Building a community around your news portal is not just about attracting readers but also about nurturing meaningful interactions and relationships. In this section, we will delve into strategies for building a strong and engaged community:

1. Audience Engagement Platforms

- **Comment Sections**: Foster constructive discussions in the comment sections of your articles by actively participating and moderating as needed.

- **Forums**: Create dedicated forums or discussion boards on your portal for readers to connect, ask questions, and share insights.

2. Newsletters and Subscriptions

- **Exclusive Content**: Offer exclusive content or early access to subscribers to incentivize sign-ups for your newsletters.

- **Personalization**: Tailor newsletters to specific subscriber interests or behaviors to enhance engagement.

3. User-Generated Content (UGC)

- **Reader Contributions**: Encourage readers to submit their stories, opinions, or photos related to news events, showcasing user-generated content on your portal.

- **Contests and Challenges**: Organize contests or challenges that motivate readers to actively participate and contribute.

4. Live Events and Webinars

- **Interactive Webinars**: Host webinars featuring expert guests or in-depth discussions on news topics, allowing real-time engagement with your audience.

- **Q&A Sessions**: Conduct live Q&A sessions with your journalists or experts to address reader questions and concerns.

5. Social Media Communities

- **Facebook Groups**: Create Facebook groups related to your news niche, where readers can discuss stories, share opinions, and interact with your team.

- **Twitter Chats**: Organize regular Twitter chats around trending news topics, inviting readers and experts to participate.

6. Membership Programs

- **Premium Membership**: Offer premium memberships with added benefits like ad-free browsing, access to exclusive content, or VIP community privileges.

- **Member-Only Events**: Host virtual or physical events exclusively for members to enhance their sense of belonging.

7. Accessibility and Inclusivity

- **Accessibility Features**: Ensure that your community platforms and content are accessible to individuals with disabilities, including screen readers and captioning.

- **Diverse Representation**: Promote inclusivity within your community by actively seeking and highlighting diverse voices and perspectives.

8. Moderation and Guidelines

- **Community Guidelines**: Establish clear community guidelines that outline expected behaviors and consequences for violations.

- **Moderation Team**: Appoint a dedicated moderation team to enforce guidelines and maintain a respectful and safe environment.

9. Recognition and Rewards

- **Top Contributors**: Recognize and reward top community contributors, fostering healthy competition and motivation.

- **Badges and Achievements**: Implement a badge or achievement system for members who reach specific milestones or contributions.

10. Feedback and Improvement

- **Feedback Channels**: Create channels for community members to provide feedback on your portal's content, design, and user experience.

- **Iterative Changes**: Act on feedback by making iterative improvements based on community input.

11. Ethical Considerations

- **Fact-Checking**: Ensure that community-contributed content adheres to ethical standards and fact-checking processes.

- **Transparency**: Be transparent about your role in moderating discussions and handling user-generated content.

12. Crisis Management

- **Community Communication**: Establish a crisis communication plan to address any community-related crises or controversies promptly and transparently.

- **Respectful Dialogue**: Promote respectful dialogue even in challenging or divisive discussions, encouraging constructive exchanges.

Building a thriving community around your news portal can enhance reader engagement, loyalty, and trust. By implementing these strategies and maintaining an open and inclusive atmosphere, you can create a vibrant and supportive community that enhances your news portal's impact.

Section 14.3: Analyzing Data and Metrics
Leveraging Insights for Growth

Harnessing Data for Success

Data analysis is a fundamental aspect of refining your news portal's strategies and understanding how your audience interacts with your content. In this section, we will delve into the ways to effectively analyze data and metrics:

1. Web Analytics Tools

- **Google Analytics**: Set up Google Analytics to track user behavior on your news portal, including page views, session durations, and user demographics.

- **Heatmaps**: Utilize heatmaps to visualize where users click and how they navigate your pages, providing insights into user engagement.

2. Audience Segmentation

- **Demographics**: Analyze the demographics of your audience, including age, gender, location, and interests, to tailor content accordingly.

- **Behavioral Segmentation**: Segment your audience based on behavior, such as frequent visitors, new users, or engaged readers, to target them effectively.

3. Content Performance

- **Top-Performing Content**: Identify your most popular articles, topics, or multimedia content to replicate successful themes.

- **Bounce Rates**: Monitor bounce rates to assess which pages might require improvements in content or user experience.

4. Engagement Metrics

- **Time on Page**: Analyze how long users spend on specific articles to gauge reader interest and content depth.

- **Comments and Shares**: Track the number of comments, social media shares, and engagement on your articles to measure their impact.

5. Conversion Tracking

- **Goal Setting**: Define conversion goals, such as newsletter sign-ups or subscription purchases, and track their completion.

- **Conversion Paths**: Analyze the paths users take to achieve conversion goals, optimizing content and user journeys accordingly.

6. A/B Testing

- **Headline Testing**: Conduct A/B tests on article headlines to determine which titles drive higher click-through rates.

- **Visual Variations**: Test different visuals or layouts to discover which designs resonate best with your audience.

7. User Feedback and Surveys

- **User Surveys**: Collect user feedback through surveys or feedback forms to gain insights into user preferences and pain points.

- **Qualitative Insights**: Analyze qualitative feedback to understand the qualitative aspects of user experiences.

8. Social Media Analytics

- **Social Media Insights**: Use the built-in analytics tools on social media platforms to gauge the reach and engagement of your social media content.

- **Referral Traffic**: Monitor the traffic generated from social media channels to assess their impact on your portal's growth.

9. Email Marketing Analytics

- **Email Open Rates**: Track email open rates to assess the effectiveness of your email campaigns and subject lines.

- **Click-Through Rates**: Analyze the click-through rates on email links to understand reader interests.

10. Data-Driven Decisions
Iterative Improvements: Use data to make iterative improvements to your content strategy, design, and user experience.

- **Content Calendar Planning**: Plan your content calendar based on data-driven insights into when your audience is most active and engaged.

11. Ethical Considerations

- **Data Privacy**: Ensure compliance with data privacy regulations and maintain transparency in data collection and usage.

- **User Consent**: Seek user consent for data collection and clearly explain how their data will be used.

12. Crisis Monitoring

- **Data Response**: Implement a data response plan to monitor data related to crisis situations or controversial content, allowing for rapid adjustments.

- **User Sentiment Analysis**: Use sentiment analysis tools to gauge public sentiment during crisis events.

By consistently analyzing data and metrics, you can make data-informed decisions that drive the growth and improvement of your news portal. These insights will guide your content creation, audience engagement strategies, and promotional efforts, ultimately enhancing the impact of your news portal.

Chapter 15: Leveraging Social Media for Your News Portal

Section 15.1: Advantages of Integrating Social Media

Unlocking the Power of Social Media

Social media integration is a potent strategy for amplifying your news portal's reach, enhancing user engagement, and providing real-time updates and interaction. In this section, we will delve into the advantages of leveraging social media for your news portal:

1. Exploring the Reach of Social Media

Reaching a Global Audience

Social media platforms provide an unprecedented opportunity to extend your news portal's reach far beyond your website's boundaries. Here's how:

- **Global Audience**: Social media platforms boast billions of active users worldwide, offering access to diverse and geographically dispersed audiences.

- **Targeted Outreach**: Utilize platform-specific features like hashtags, groups, and pages to target users with specific interests or demographics.

- **Viral Potential**: Create shareable content that has the potential to go viral, allowing your stories to spread rapidly across social networks.

2. Increasing User Engagement

Fostering Community and Dialogue

Social media is a fertile ground for nurturing user engagement and fostering meaningful conversations with your audience:

- **Interactive Communication**: Engage with your readers through comments, direct messages, and polls, creating a sense of community and dialogue around your news.

- **Feedback Loop**: Social media platforms enable direct feedback, allowing you to gain insights into reader opinions, concerns, and preferences.

- **Prompt Response**: Respond to reader comments and inquiries promptly, demonstrating your commitment to engaging with your audience.

3. Real-time Updates and Interaction

Timely Reporting and Interaction

The real-time nature of social media makes it an invaluable tool for delivering news updates and facilitating interaction:

- **Live Reporting**: Utilize live video streaming to provide real-time reporting during events, protests, or breaking news, offering an immersive experience to your audience.

- **Live Q&A Sessions**: Conduct live question-and-answer sessions with experts or journalists to provide insights and interact directly with your audience.

- **Timely Alerts**: Share critical updates, alerts, and emergency information quickly and efficiently during crises or significant news events.

- **User-Generated Content**: Encourage users to submit photos, videos, and eyewitness accounts during major events, enhancing your portal's coverage.

Social media's reach, engagement capabilities, and real-time features empower your news portal to connect with a broader audience, encourage active participation, and deliver news as it unfolds. By harnessing these advantages, you can establish a dynamic and influential presence in the digital news landscape.

Section 15.2: How to Effectively Use Social Media

Strategies for Success

Effectively using social media as part of your news portal strategy involves selecting the right platforms, creating shareable content, and engaging your audience in a meaningful way. In this section, we will delve into these strategies:

1. Choosing the Right Platforms

Matching Platforms to Your Goals

Selecting the appropriate social media platforms is crucial for reaching your target audience and achieving your news portal's goals:

- **Audience Research**: Conduct thorough audience research to understand where your target demographic is most active. Different platforms cater to distinct age groups and interests.

- **Platform Suitability**: Assess which platforms align with your content format. For visual content, platforms like Instagram and Pinterest may be more suitable, while Twitter and LinkedIn are better for sharing news articles and analysis.

- **Platform Popularity**: Consider the popularity of platforms in your specific news niche. Some platforms may have a more significant presence for certain topics or industries.

2. Crafting Shareable Content

Engaging and Viral-Worthy Content

Creating content that resonates with your audience and encourages sharing is essential for maximizing your news portal's social media impact:

- **Headlines and Hooks**: Craft attention-grabbing headlines and hooks that compel users to click and engage with your content.

- **Visual Appeal**: Use high-quality visuals, including images, infographics, and videos, to make your content more shareable and visually appealing.

- **Storytelling**: Embrace storytelling techniques to make your articles more relatable and emotionally engaging for readers.

- **Timeliness**: Share breaking news and trending topics promptly to leverage current events for increased visibility.

3. Building and Engaging Your Audience

Fostering Relationships and Loyalty

Building a loyal and engaged social media following requires consistent effort and genuine interaction:

- **Regular Posting**: Maintain a consistent posting schedule to keep your audience engaged and informed. Use content calendars to plan and organize posts.

- **Community Engagement**: Respond to comments, messages, and mentions promptly. Acknowledge and appreciate your audience's contributions and feedback.

- **Polls and Surveys**: Use polls and surveys to involve your audience in decision-making or gather opinions on relevant topics.

- **Contests and Challenges**: Organize contests or challenges that encourage user participation and content creation related to your news niche.

- **Collaborations**: Collaborate with other social media influencers, news outlets, or experts to cross-promote content and tap into their audience.

- **Analytics and Insights**: Regularly review social media analytics to understand what type of content resonates with your audience. Adjust your strategy accordingly.

- **Feedback and User-Generated Content**: Encourage your audience to share their stories, opinions, and experiences related to news events. Showcase user-generated content on your social media profiles.

By selecting the right platforms, crafting shareable content, and actively engaging your audience, you can harness the full potential of social media for your news portal. These strategies will help you expand your reach, build a loyal readership, and foster a thriving online community around your news content.

Section 15.3: Leveraging Paid Advertising

Strategic Advertising on Social Media

Paid advertising on social media can be a powerful tool to enhance your news portal's visibility and engagement. In this section, we will delve into the strategies and considerations for leveraging paid advertising effectively:

1. Targeted Advertising Campaigns

Reaching Your Ideal Audience

Running targeted advertising campaigns on social media ensures that your content reaches the most relevant audience segments:

- **Audience Segmentation**: Use platform-specific targeting options to narrow down your audience by demographics, interests, behaviors, and location.

- **Custom Audiences**: Create custom audience segments based on user interactions with your portal, such as website visits or engagement with previous ads.

- **Lookalike Audiences**: Expand your reach by creating lookalike audiences that mimic the characteristics of your existing audience base.

- **Ad Formats**: Choose ad formats that align with your campaign goals, whether it's promoting articles, videos, or driving newsletter sign-ups.

2. Measuring ROI on Social Media Ads

Evaluating Advertising Effectiveness

Measuring the return on investment (ROI) of your social media advertising campaigns is essential for optimizing your spending:

- **Key Performance Indicators (KPIs)**: Define clear KPIs for your campaigns, such as click-through rates, conversion rates, or cost per acquisition.

- **Tracking Pixels**: Implement tracking pixels on your portal to monitor user actions after clicking on ads, providing insights into conversion paths.

- **A/B Testing**: Conduct A/B tests to evaluate different ad creatives, headlines, and targeting options to determine what works best.

- **Conversion Attribution**: Understand how different touchpoints contribute to conversions, including view-through and click-through attribution.

- **Ad Spend Analysis**: Regularly review your ad spend and adjust budgets based on the performance of individual campaigns.

3. Avoiding Common Pitfalls

Steering Clear of Mistakes

While paid advertising can yield substantial benefits, it's important to be aware of common pitfalls and challenges:

- **Ad Fatigue**: Be cautious of showing the same ads to your audience too frequently, which can lead to ad fatigue and decreased engagement.

- **Budget Management**: Set clear budgets for your campaigns and avoid overspending. Monitor your ad spend regularly to ensure it aligns with your goals.

- **Misalignment with Audience**: Ensure your ad messaging and visuals align with the expectations and interests of your target audience.

- **Ad Transparency**: Clearly label sponsored content as advertising to maintain transparency and credibility.

- **Ad Relevance**: Continuously assess the relevance of your ad campaigns to your news content and the interests of your audience.

- **Ad Copy and Design**: Invest time in crafting compelling ad copy and eye-catching visuals to maximize the effectiveness of your ads.

By running targeted advertising campaigns, measuring ROI, and avoiding common pitfalls, you can harness the potential of paid advertising on social media to expand your news portal's reach and engagement. These strategies will enable you to make data-informed decisions and allocate your advertising budget effectively.

Section 15.4: Managing Social Media Crisis

Navigating Troubling Waters

In the digital age, social media can be both a boon and a challenge. Handling social media crises effectively is crucial to maintaining your news portal's reputation and credibility. In this section, we will delve into strategies for managing social media crises:

1. Handling Negative Feedback

Turning Criticism into Opportunity

Negative feedback and criticism are inevitable on social media. How you handle it can make a significant difference:

- **Prompt Responses**: Respond to negative comments and feedback promptly and professionally. Acknowledge concerns and address them constructively.

- **Constructive Dialogue**: Engage in constructive conversations with users, aiming to find solutions and common ground.

- **Private Communication**: In cases where issues require detailed discussion, encourage users to reach out privately through direct messages or emails.

2. Addressing Fake News and Misinformation

Fighting the Spread of Falsehoods

News portals have a responsibility to combat the spread of fake news and misinformation:

- **Fact-Checking**: Implement rigorous fact-checking processes to ensure the accuracy of your news content.

- **Immediate Corrections**: If errors are identified, correct them promptly and transparently, providing clear information on what was incorrect.

- **Dispute False Claims**: If your portal is falsely accused of spreading misinformation, address these claims with verifiable evidence.

3. Strategies for Crisis Communication

Being Prepared and Proactive

223

Developing a crisis communication strategy is essential to navigate difficult situations effectively:

- **Preparation**: Anticipate potential crisis scenarios and develop response plans in advance.

- **Transparency**: Communicate openly and honestly with your audience during crises, providing updates and relevant information.

- **Spokesperson**: Designate a spokesperson who can represent your portal professionally and consistently.

- **Monitoring Tools**: Utilize social media monitoring tools to track mentions and sentiment related to your portal in real-time.

- **Crisis Response Team**: Assemble a team responsible for managing crises, including PR professionals, legal experts, and communication specialists.

- **Consistent Messaging**: Ensure that messages across all social media platforms and your news portal are consistent in tone and content.

- **Apologies and Corrective Actions**: When appropriate, issue sincere apologies and outline corrective actions your portal will take.

- **Post-Crisis Evaluation**: After the crisis has been resolved, conduct a thorough evaluation to identify lessons learned and areas for improvement in your crisis management strategy.

Effectively managing social media crises requires a combination of proactive planning, transparent communication, and a commitment to maintaining the integrity of your news portal. By addressing negative feedback, combating misinformation, and implementing crisis communication strategies, you can navigate challenging situations while upholding your portal's reputation.

Section 15.5: Future Trends in Social Media Integration

Staying Ahead of the Curve

Staying informed about emerging trends and challenges in social media integration is essential for the long-term success of your news portal. In this section, we will delve into future trends and considerations:

1. Embracing Emerging Platforms

Expanding Your Digital Footprint

Social media is an ever-evolving landscape with new platforms constantly emerging. Here's how you can stay ahead:

- **Platform Exploration**: Continuously explore emerging social media platforms to assess their relevance to your audience and content.

- **Early Adoption**: Consider early adoption of promising platforms to establish a presence before they become saturated.

- **Targeted Testing**: Run small-scale campaigns or content experiments on emerging platforms to gauge audience response.

- **User Demographics**: Analyze the demographics and interests of users on new platforms to determine alignment with your news niche.

2. The Role of AI in Social Media Marketing

Automating and Enhancing Engagement

Artificial intelligence (AI) is revolutionizing social media marketing. Understand how AI can benefit your news portal:

- **Content Recommendations**: Implement AI algorithms to suggest personalized content to users based on their preferences and behavior.

- **Chatbots and Automation**: Use AI-powered chatbots to provide instant responses to user queries and automate routine tasks like content posting and scheduling.

- **Data Analysis**: Leverage AI for in-depth data analysis, helping you identify trends, sentiment, and user behavior for more effective content strategies.

- **Predictive Analytics**: Utilize AI-driven predictive analytics to forecast audience engagement and optimize content creation.

3. Navigating Regulatory Challenges

Compliance and Ethics

As social media continues to evolve, regulatory challenges may arise. Ensure you navigate them effectively:

- **Privacy Regulations**: Stay updated on privacy regulations, such as GDPR or CCPA, and ensure your social media practices comply with data protection laws.

- **Content Moderation**: Develop content moderation guidelines to address issues like hate speech, misinformation, and user-generated content that violates community standards.

- **Ethical Journalism**: Uphold ethical journalism standards on social media by verifying sources, fact-checking, and avoiding sensationalism.

- **Transparency**: Maintain transparency in sponsored content and ensure you adhere to disclosure guidelines for sponsored posts and partnerships.

- **Legal Consultation**: When in doubt, seek legal consultation to ensure your social media practices align with relevant laws and regulations.

Staying informed about emerging platforms, embracing AI-driven strategies, and navigating regulatory challenges will enable your news portal to remain competitive and adaptable in the ever-evolving landscape of social media integration.

Chapter 16: Insights from the News Portal Industry

Section 16.1: Case Studies of Successful News Portals

Learning from Industry Leaders

Analyzing the strategies and journeys of successful news portals can provide valuable insights for your own endeavors. In this section, we will delve into case studies of three prominent news portals:

1. Examining the Success of "NewsHub"

Breaking New Ground

"NewsHub" is a prime example of a news portal that has achieved remarkable success. Let's explore the factors contributing to its triumph:

- **Niche Focus**: "NewsHub" strategically chose a specific news niche, focusing on in-depth analysis and breaking news related to technology and innovation.

- **Quality Journalism**: The portal prioritized quality journalism by investing in experienced journalists and subject matter experts, ensuring accurate and engaging content.

- **Audience Engagement**: "NewsHub" actively engaged with its audience through comment sections, social media, and newsletters, fostering a strong sense of community.

- **Visual Storytelling**: The portal embraced multimedia content, including videos, infographics, and interactive articles, enhancing the overall user experience.

- **Monetization Strategies**: "NewsHub" implemented a variety of monetization strategies, including subscription models, sponsored content, and targeted advertising.

2. The Impactful Journey of "Global Insights"

A Global Perspective

"Global Insights" carved its path to success with a focus on global news and perspectives. Let's uncover the elements that contributed to its impact:

- **Diverse Content**: "Global Insights" featured a diverse range of content, including international politics, culture, and human interest stories, attracting a broad and engaged audience.

- **Multilingual Approach**: Recognizing the global nature of its audience, the portal offered content in multiple languages, making it accessible to a wider readership.

- **Community Building**: "Global Insights" fostered an active online community where readers could share their thoughts and perspectives, creating a sense of belonging.

- **Collaborations**: The portal collaborated with international news agencies and correspondents, providing exclusive insights and breaking news from around the world.

- **Adaptive Business Model**: "Global Insights" continuously adapted its business model, incorporating paywalls for premium content and exploring sponsorship opportunities.

3. Lessons from "TechTalk Daily"

Tech-Centric Excellence

"TechTalk Daily" made a significant impact in the tech news niche. Let's uncover the key lessons to learn from its journey:

- **Niche Expertise**: "TechTalk Daily" established itself as an authority in technology reporting, with a team of tech-savvy journalists and industry experts.

- **Timely Coverage**: The portal consistently delivered timely and in-depth coverage of tech trends, product launches, and industry insights, keeping readers informed.

- **Engaging Formats**: "TechTalk Daily" experimented with various content formats, including podcasts, webinars, and live Q&A sessions, increasing user engagement.

- **User-Generated Content**: The portal encouraged user-generated content, allowing tech enthusiasts to contribute articles, reviews, and opinions.

- **Monetization Innovation**: "TechTalk Daily" explored innovative monetization models, such as premium memberships with exclusive access to tech events and content.

By examining the success stories of "NewsHub," "Global Insights," and "TechTalk Daily," you can gain valuable insights into niche-focused strategies, audience engagement, and innovative monetization models. These case studies offer inspiration and lessons that you can apply to your own news portal journey.

Section 16.2: Lessons from Closed Popular Portals

Understanding the Pitfalls

Examining the experiences of closed popular news portals can provide valuable lessons in what to avoid. In this section, we will delve into the stories of three notable portals:

1. Analyzing the Downfall of "BreakingNewsNow"

A Cautionary Tale

"BreakingNewsNow" was once a prominent news portal that faced challenges leading to its closure. Let's explore the factors that contributed to its downfall:

- **Lack of Diversification**: "BreakingNewsNow" primarily focused on breaking news, neglecting to diversify its content to cater to broader interests.

- **Monetization Struggles**: The portal heavily relied on advertising revenue and couldn't effectively adapt to changing ad industry trends and ad-blocker usage.

- **Quality vs. Quantity**: Emphasizing speed over accuracy led to credibility issues, ultimately eroding trust among its audience.

- **Competition**: The portal faced stiff competition from other news outlets, making it challenging to stand out in a crowded market.

- **Innovation Stagnation**: "BreakingNewsNow" failed to innovate its content delivery methods, such as not embracing multimedia and interactive features.

2. The Challenges Faced by "The Citizen Times"

Navigating Turbulent Waters

"The Citizen Times" encountered significant challenges during its existence. Let's uncover the hurdles it faced:

- **Funding Shortages**: The portal struggled with funding and revenue generation, limiting its ability to invest in quality journalism and user engagement.

- **Digital Transition**: "The Citizen Times" faced difficulties transitioning from print to digital, including adapting to new storytelling formats and platforms.

- **Changing Audience Behavior**: Shifting reader preferences, including increased consumption of social media news, posed challenges in retaining and growing its audience.

- **Competition with Legacy Media**: Competing with well-established legacy media outlets made it challenging for "The Citizen Times" to gain market share.

- **Monetization Strategies**: The portal grappled with finding effective monetization strategies beyond traditional advertising.

3. Learning from Failures: "MediaWave"

Extracting Valuable Insights

"MediaWave" is a portal whose lessons from failure can guide future endeavors:

- **Editorial Independence**: "MediaWave" faced credibility issues due to perceived editorial biases, highlighting the importance of maintaining editorial independence.

- **Content Strategy**: The portal struggled with content relevance and audience engagement, emphasizing the need for a clear content strategy.

- **Resource Allocation**: "MediaWave" faced challenges in resource allocation, including investing in quality reporting and audience growth.

- **Adaptation to Trends**: Failing to adapt quickly to emerging digital trends hindered "MediaWave" in maintaining relevance.

- **User Feedback**: Ignoring user feedback and failing to address concerns led to a decline in user trust.

By analyzing the stories of "BreakingNewsNow," "The Citizen Times," and "MediaWave," you can gain valuable insights into pitfalls to avoid, such as a lack of diversification, monetization struggles, and difficulties in adapting to changing audience behavior and digital trends. Learning from these experiences will help you make informed decisions in your news portal journey.

Section 16.3: Common Mistakes to Avoid

Learning from Errors

Recognizing and avoiding common mistakes is crucial for the success of your news portal. In this section, we will delve into three prevalent mistakes:

1. Overlooking Legal and Ethical Considerations

Guardians of Integrity

Maintaining the highest legal and ethical standards is fundamental to the credibility of your news portal:

- **Copyright Infringement**: Neglecting to secure proper permissions for content usage can lead to legal issues and reputation damage.

- **Plagiarism**: Plagiarism can erode trust and damage your portal's reputation. Implement strict plagiarism checks to uphold originality.

- **Libel and Defamation**: Failing to verify facts or publishing defamatory content can result in costly legal battles and credibility loss.

- **Privacy Violations**: Mishandling user data or intruding on individuals' privacy can result in legal liabilities and regulatory fines.

- **Transparency**: Lack of transparency in content partnerships, sponsorships, or political affiliations can lead to accusations of bias and unethical practices.

2. Neglecting User Experience and Design

The Aesthetics of Engagement

User experience (UX) and design play a critical role in retaining and attracting readers:

- **Website Navigation**: Complex or cluttered navigation can frustrate users. Streamline the website layout for easy access to content.

- **Mobile Optimization**: Neglecting mobile optimization can result in a poor experience for users accessing your portal via smartphones and tablets.

- **Slow Loading Times**: Slow-loading pages can deter users. Optimize website performance to ensure swift access to content.

- **Accessibility**: Failing to make your portal accessible to users with disabilities may result in exclusion and legal consequences.

- **Visual Appeal**: Aesthetically unpleasing design can deter readers. Invest in visually appealing layouts and graphics.

3. Underestimating Content Quality

The Foundation of Trust

Content quality is the bedrock of a news portal's credibility and readership:

- **Rushed Reporting**: Prioritizing speed over accuracy can lead to misinformation and credibility damage. Balance the need for timely reporting with thorough fact-checking.

- **Sensationalism**: Overemphasizing sensational headlines or stories can erode trust. Focus on balanced, objective reporting.

- **Lack of Depth**: Shallow or clickbait content may attract short-term attention but fails to engage and retain readers in the long run.

- **Neglecting Investigative Journalism**: Failing to invest in investigative journalism can limit your portal's ability to uncover important stories.

- **Editorial Oversight**: Insufficient editorial oversight can result in biased or unverified content, compromising credibility.

By recognizing and avoiding the common mistakes of overlooking legal and ethical considerations, neglecting user experience and design, and underestimating content quality, your news portal can build a strong foundation for credibility and success. These lessons highlight the importance of ethical journalism practices, user-centric design, and high-quality content creation.

Section 16.4: Tips for New Beginners

Guidance for a Successful Start

For new beginners in the news portal industry, the following tips can pave the way for a successful journey:

1. Research and Market Analysis

Informed Decision-Making

- **Market Understanding**: Begin with comprehensive market research to identify niche opportunities and audience preferences.

- **Competitor Analysis**: Study existing news portals in your chosen niche to understand their strengths and weaknesses.

- **Audience Segmentation**: Analyze your target audience's demographics, interests, and behavior to tailor content effectively.

- **Content Gap Analysis**: Identify content gaps in the market that your portal can fill, offering unique and valuable insights.

2. Building a Strong Brand Identity

Setting Yourself Apart

- **Brand Story**: Craft a compelling brand story that defines your portal's mission, values, and unique selling proposition.

- **Logo and Visual Identity**: Create a memorable logo and visual identity that resonates with your target audience.

- **Consistent Messaging**: Maintain consistency in messaging and tone across all content and platforms to establish trust.

- **Content Voice**: Develop a distinct content voice that reflects your brand's personality and editorial stance.

- **Community Engagement**: Build a community around your brand by actively engaging with readers and responding to feedback.

3. Collaborating with Influencers and Experts

Amplifying Your Reach

- **Influencer Partnerships**: Collaborate with influencers in your niche to extend your portal's reach and credibility.

- **Expert Contributions**: Invite subject matter experts to contribute guest articles or participate in interviews, adding authority to your content.

- **Joint Ventures**: Explore partnerships and joint ventures with established news outlets or complementary businesses.

- **Networking**: Attend industry events and engage in networking to connect with potential collaborators and mentors.

4. Embracing Innovation and Adaptation

Staying Ahead of the Curve

- **Technological Innovation**: Stay updated on technological trends and consider how emerging technologies like AI and AR can enhance your portal.

- **Content Formats**: Experiment with various content formats, such as podcasts, videos, and interactive features, to engage diverse audiences.

- **Feedback Integration**: Continuously gather user feedback and adapt your portal's content and features accordingly.

- **Scalability**: Plan for scalability by building a flexible infrastructure that can accommodate growth.

- **Content Evolution**: Embrace content evolution by being open to shifts in audience interests and news consumption habits.

These tips provide new beginners in the news portal industry with valuable guidance for navigating the challenges and opportunities that come with launching and growing a successful portal. By conducting thorough research, establishing a strong brand identity, collaborating strategically, and staying innovative and adaptable, you can position your news portal for long-term success.

Chapter 17: Conclusion and Future Directions

As you near the end of your journey in news portal publishing, it's crucial to reflect on your accomplishments and chart a path for the future. This chapter provides insights on concluding your current phase and preparing for what lies ahead.

Section 17.1: Reflecting on Your Journey

Looking Back to Move Forward

As you approach the conclusion of your journey in news portal publishing, taking the time to reflect on your experiences and the impact you've made is essential for growth and future success.

Assessing Achievements

Recognizing Milestones

- **Content Milestones**: Evaluate the quality and quantity of content produced over time. Celebrate the publication of significant stories, investigative reports, or exclusive interviews.

- **Audience Growth**: Analyze the growth of your readership, considering factors like unique visitors, page views, and engagement metrics.

- **Awards and Recognition**: Recognize any awards, accolades, or industry recognition your portal has received for outstanding journalism.

- **Monetization Success**: If you've implemented revenue streams, assess the success of your monetization efforts, such as advertising revenue, subscription models, or sponsored content.

Learning from Challenges

Turning Obstacles into Opportunities

- **Technical Challenges**: Reflect on any technical issues or disruptions your portal faced and how you successfully resolved them. Identify areas where your technical infrastructure can be strengthened.

- **Content Challenges**: Consider instances where content creation or publication presented challenges and the strategies you employed to overcome them.

- **Adaptation to Trends**: Reflect on how your portal adapted to changing industry trends, such as shifts in reader behavior or emerging storytelling formats.

- **Resource Management**: Evaluate how effectively you managed your resources, including budget, human capital, and time, to navigate challenges.

Gauging Impact

Measuring Your Influence

- **Audience Reach**: Assess the reach of your news portal by analyzing geographic distribution, user demographics, and the extent of your global audience.

- **Social and Civic Impact**: Reflect on the social and civic impact of your reporting. Consider whether your news stories led to positive change or influenced public discourse.

- **Community Engagement**: Gauge your portal's engagement with local and global communities, including partnerships, events, or initiatives that promoted civic engagement and social responsibility.

User Feedback

Listening to Your Readers

- **Feedback Channels**: Review the feedback channels you established, such as comment sections, surveys, or social media interactions, to understand user sentiment and preferences.

- **Patterns and Trends**: Identify patterns and trends in user feedback. Are there recurring themes or suggestions for improvement that you can address?

- **User-Centric Improvements**: Use user feedback to inform improvements in user experience, content selection, and overall portal design.

- **Enhancement Opportunities**: Determine areas where user feedback indicates room for enhancement or innovation, whether in content delivery, features, or services.

By thoroughly assessing your achievements, learning from challenges, gauging your portal's impact, and actively listening to user feedback, you can gain valuable insights that will not only help you celebrate your journey but also pave the way for future growth and success in news portal publishing.

Section 17.2: Adapting to Changing Trends

Navigating the Shifting Landscape

In the ever-evolving landscape of news portal publishing, staying adaptable and responsive to changing trends is paramount for long-term success.

Trend Analysis

Informed Decision-Making

- **Ongoing Market Research**: Commit to ongoing market research to stay informed about industry trends and shifts in reader preferences. Monitor competitor strategies and emerging news formats.

- **Data-Driven Insights**: Leverage data analytics tools to gain actionable insights from user behavior, engagement metrics, and content performance. Use these insights to guide editorial decisions.

- **Reader Surveys**: Conduct regular reader surveys to understand audience expectations and gather direct feedback on content preferences, usability, and overall user experience.

- **Collaborative Efforts**: Collaborate with market research firms, industry associations, or academic institutions to gain a deeper understanding of broader media trends.

Technology Integration

Enhancing Capabilities

- **AI and Automation**: Embrace the potential of AI-driven technologies for content creation, recommendation systems, and personalized user experiences. Implement automation to streamline routine tasks.

- **Immersive Storytelling**: Explore immersive storytelling tools, such as virtual reality (VR) or augmented reality (AR), to provide unique and engaging news experiences.

- **Mobile Optimization**: Prioritize mobile optimization to ensure that your portal functions seamlessly on various devices, including smartphones and tablets.

- **Adaptive Design**: Implement responsive design principles to create a fluid and adaptable user interface that adjusts to different screen sizes and resolutions.

User-Centric Approach

Prioritizing User Satisfaction

- **User Behavior Analysis**: Continuously analyze user behavior and adapt your portal to changing user preferences. Keep a close eye on shifts in the platforms and devices your audience uses.

- **Responsive Design**: Ensure that your portal provides a seamless and user-friendly experience across multiple platforms and screen sizes.

- **Feedback Loops**: Establish feedback loops with your audience through surveys, comment sections, and social media. Use this feedback to make user-centric improvements.

- **Accessibility**: Commit to accessibility standards to ensure that all users, including those with disabilities, can access and engage with your content.

Content Evolution

Remaining Relevant

- **Content Formats**: Be open to evolving your content strategy to embrace emerging news formats, such as podcasts, video news, interactive graphics, and data journalism.

- **Audience Interests**: Regularly assess audience interests and adapt your content to cater to their evolving needs and expectations. Consider what topics and formats resonate most with your readers.

- **Experimentation**: Encourage experimentation within your editorial team to explore new storytelling techniques and formats that align with changing trends.

- **Quality Assurance**: Maintain high standards of content quality and accuracy, even as you experiment with new formats. Fact-checking and editorial rigor remain essential.

By actively engaging in trend analysis, integrating relevant technologies, adopting a user-centric approach, and evolving your content to match audience interests, you can position your news portal as a dynamic and forward-looking platform that continues to thrive in a rapidly changing media landscape.

Section 17.3: Continuing to Innovate

Fostering a Culture of Innovation

To thrive in the ever-changing landscape of news portal publishing, cultivating a culture of innovation within your organization is crucial.

Innovation Culture

Cultivating Creativity

- **Encourage Creativity**: Create an environment where team members feel empowered to think creatively and propose innovative ideas. Foster a culture where risk-taking is seen as a part of growth.

- **Diverse Perspectives**: Promote diversity within your team, as different perspectives and backgrounds can lead to more innovative solutions and storytelling approaches.

- **Innovation Challenges**: Host innovation challenges or brainstorming sessions to actively seek out and nurture innovative concepts and projects.

Team Development

Equipping Your Team

- **Continuous Learning**: Invest in the professional development of your team members by providing access to training, workshops, and courses that enhance their skills in journalism, technology, and digital media.

- **Cross-Training**: Encourage cross-training among team members to expand their knowledge and skill sets. This can lead to fresh insights and collaborative problem-solving.

- **Innovation Training**: Offer specific innovation training programs to equip your team with the tools and techniques needed to stay at the forefront of news portal innovation.

Collaboration

Strengthening Partnerships

- **Media Collaborations**: Explore partnerships and collaborations with other media outlets, both traditional and digital, to leverage shared resources, reach wider audiences, and collaborate on investigative projects.

- **Technology Partnerships**: Forge partnerships with technology companies and startups that can provide innovative tools and solutions for news gathering, content delivery, and audience engagement.

- **Journalism Innovators**: Engage with journalism innovators, such as journalism schools, research institutions, and tech-driven news organizations, to exchange ideas and best practices.

Reader Engagement

Fostering a Feedback Loop

- **Feedback Channels**: Maintain and expand feedback channels with your audience, including surveys, social media interactions, and online forums. Actively seek their input on new features or content formats.

- **Audience-Led Initiatives**: Encourage reader-generated content and initiatives, such as user-generated stories, citizen journalism, or community-driven reporting.

- **Audience Communities**: Build and nurture online communities and forums where readers can engage with each other and provide valuable insights.

Sustainability

Long-Term Viability

- **Diversified Revenue Streams**: Explore diversified revenue streams beyond traditional advertising, such as subscription models, memberships, sponsored content, events, or merchandise sales.

- **Ethical Considerations**: Ensure that your revenue models align with your portal's mission and values, upholding ethical journalism standards while generating income.

- **Business Model Innovation**: Continually assess and refine your business model to adapt to changing market dynamics and reader expectations.

- **Environmental Responsibility**: Consider the environmental impact of your operations and explore sustainable practices, such as reducing carbon footprints and responsible sourcing.

By fostering a culture of innovation, investing in team development, seeking collaborations, engaging with readers, and ensuring long-term sustainability, your news portal can remain dynamic and responsive in a rapidly evolving media landscape. This commitment to innovation and adaptation will help you continue to deliver impactful journalism and engage with your audience effectively.

Recommended Books

The Complete Guide to

INVESTIGATIVE JOURNALISM

A Handbook for Candidate and
New - Beginner Journalists

OSMAN KARAKAS
Award-winning Journalist & Lecturer

A COMPREHENSIVE AND
PRACTICAL GUIDEBOOK

News Writing Techniques

MOST COMMON MISTAKES AND TIPS

OSMAN KARAKAS
AWARD-WINNING JOURNALIST & LECTURER

PROFESSIONAL PHOTO JOURNALISM

A Comprehensive Study Guide
for Professional Journalists
OSMAN KARAKAS
Award-winning Journalist & Lecturer

THE SOCIAL MEDIA PARADOX

Citizen Journalism or
Social Media Terror?

OSMAN KARAKAS
AWARD-WINNING JOURNALIST & LECTURER

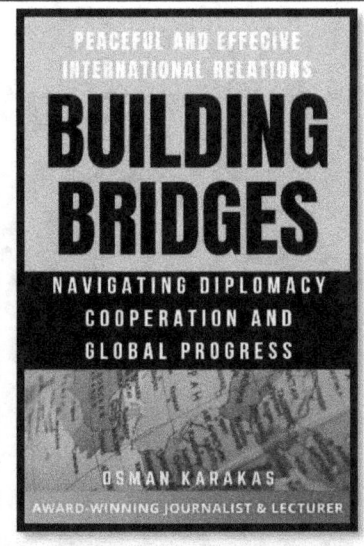

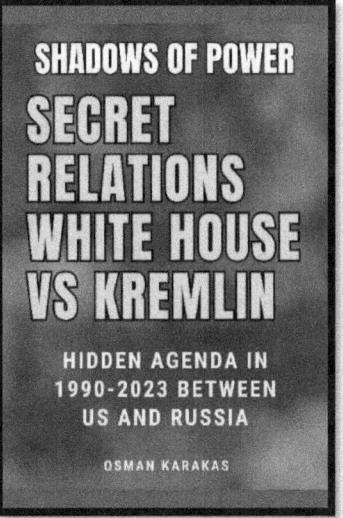

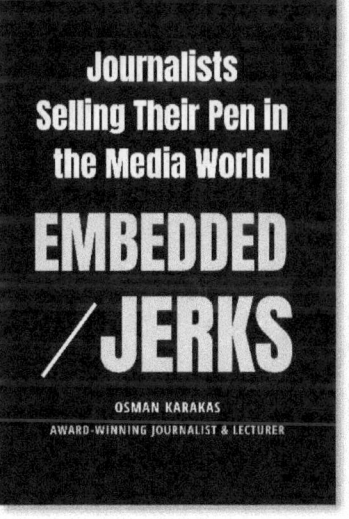

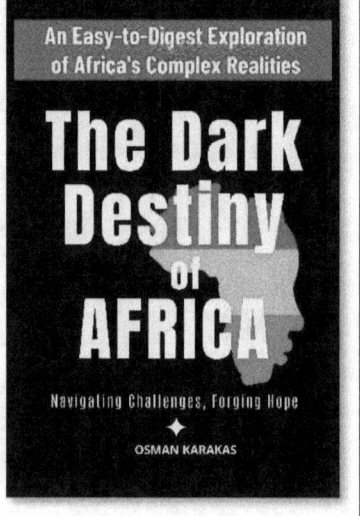

The collection of books is accessible for purchase on Amazon.com platform.